The Baby Boom:
Making Sense of Our Generation at Forty

The Baby Boom: Making Sense of Our Generation at Forty

JOHN PARIKHAL

Copyright © 1993 John Parikhal
Published in North America by
Joint Communications Corporation
Publishing Division
90 Burnhamthorpe Road West
Suite 410
Mississauga, Ontario
L5B 3C3
Canada
Fax: 416-272-5258

Although the author and publisher have made every effort to ensure the accuracy and completeness of information contained in this book, we assume no responsibility for errors, inaccuracies, omissions, or any inconsistency herein. Any slight of people, places, or organizations is unintentional.

Canadian Cataloguing in Publication Data

Parikhal, John
The baby boom : making sense of our generation at forty
ISBN   0-9696488-0-4
1.   Middle age.   2.   Aging—Social aspects.
3.   Lif

HQ1059.4.P37 1993   305.24 '4   C92-090824-9

Project Management & Design: Paula Chabanais & Associates Limited, Canada.

Printed in Canada

Contents

To John McGhan

Acknowledgments

This book was made possible by the kind help and honest advice of many people. Each one contributed something special, helping to strengthen and shape an idea into a manuscript, and then a book.

I would like to extend my thanks and sincere appreciation to many of those who helped make this book possible:
— to my wife Pat, whose support was essential as I balanced a full-time job and a writing career;
— to John McGhan, who helped me focus on the essence of the Baby Boom at forty when I was drowning in statistics;
— to my friends and colleagues who read and improved the manuscript: Allan Gregg, Steve Berger, Nick Saab, Robert Tucker, Tom Freston, Dave Charles, Bob Wilson, Beverley Beetham Endersby, and my father and mother;
— to my literary agent, Lucinda Vardey, who tirelessly suggested editorial improvements while pushing me to write more of my own life as a Baby Boomer into the book. Lucinda's faith in the manuscript got me through;
— to Harvey Galloway and Steve Sedlak, from Nationwide Insurance, who provided the actuarial calculations;

— to Michael Shalett and Michael Fine from Sound Data for all the music and entertainment research;

— to my staff at Joint Communications who worked long and hard to get *The Baby Boom* to press;

— to the many supporters who have encouraged this work in progress for the past four years; and

— to my daughter, Lauren, who reminds me every day that life begins at forty.

Erratum

Page ix, line one should read "700,000" instead of "700,00".

Prologue

More than 700,00 Baby Boomers will live to be one hundred years old! Most of them will be women. They will be preceded by more than 8 million Baby Boom women who will live to be ninety. And they will be joined by 3 million Baby Boom men.

These startling statistics are one more example of the enormous size and social impact of our "Big Generation." The Baby Boom is aging. As it moves toward its hundredth birthday, it simultaneously redefines an important landmark for this youth-obsessed generation—age forty.

As we age, forty is shedding its baggage as a symbol of decline, decay, and general winding down. Instead, it is being reinvigorated as a second starting point for a generation that has experimented, challenged, and made its presence felt at every stage of its collective life. Things will be no different as we turn forty. Our experimentation will continue to challenge everything with which we come in contact. This book will explain how and why.

It will help us realize we are not as weird as we thought. It will explain why our so-called selfishness is a critical survival skill. And to satisfy our curiosity, it will let us compare ourselves to other forty-year-olds on a wide range of issues such as sex, regrets, family, and even our attitudes toward our jobs.

Let's start with the fact that, for all Baby Boomers, there's good news about turning forty.

We haven't started listening to Muzak. We don't need dentures. And we think about sex as much as we ever did, even if we don't get around to it quite as often.

In fact, we don't think forty is old. We haven't settled into a comfortable middle age, gazing at the TV and waiting for our old-age-pension checks to arrive. Instead, we look young, act young, and feel young.

But in spite of our youthful feeling, we approach forty in much the same way that a caveman would have approached a saber-toothed tiger — with a mixture of awe, dread, and admiration for its enormous power. And, just as the caveman believed he could conquer the tiger, we bravely tackle forty.

So, we experience contradiction. We feel young, but, for the first time, we are conscious of our age. We feel good now, but we fear feeling bad later.

Each of us approaches forty in a different state of mind: For each of us, forty holds a special set of expectations, hopes, and fears.

Some of us are just plain curious. What will it be like? Is it really such a big deal? How are other forty-year-olds dealing with aging? What lies ahead?

Others are just plain scared. What will I do without my youth? How can I deal with the bags, sags, and folds of my face and body? Why can't I stay young forever?

A third group is confused. What should I do with my life now? How can I bundle all of my experience into something useful and turn the next half of my life into something joyful? Why do I feel so strange?

Of course, there are the cavalier, "I-don't-give-a-damn-about-anything" types as well. What's the big deal about forty? I've made it this far, so I'll just keep going.

Finally, there are those who view forty as an important milestone, a benchmark for taking stock of the past and an opportunity to use this insight to make the next forty years better than the last forty.

After all, as members of the Baby Boom we are a generation of optimists, of self-improvers and fad-followers. At the same time, we are the smartest generation in history, the best educated. This optimism and education combine to create a potent formula that can turn a fortieth birthday into a milestone on the road to a better life.

The Baby Boom: Making Sense of Our Generation at Forty takes a snapshot of our generation at this milestone. It probes, analyzes, illuminates, and has fun with a generation who have reshaped our society as they moved through it, like a pig through a python, creating a noticeable bulge and unavoidable impact wherever we went. Most Baby Boomer observers have focused on the obvious — our effect on the educational system, our penchant for social protest, and our impact on housing prices. The doom-sayers suggest that we will bankrupt Social Security and end our days fighting for space in nursing homes. The optimists think that we will use the collectivism we experienced during the sixties and early seventies to solve most of the social problems we are creating. This book provides answers to questions about the direction we are likely to take.

It is a fact-filled romp through our collective experience, touching on the things that we loved, such as the Beatles; the things that changed us forever, such as the Vietnam War; and the things that are taking on a new, practical urgency, such as concerns about pensions and health.

The Baby Boom is based on facts — specifically, on the facts gathered in a survey of thousands of forty-year-olds — and is meant to be illuminating, funny, and full of useful information. It tries to make sense of midlife, explaining how we got to where we are and exploring where we may be going, at the same time providing practical advice and insight.

If you want to get into the heavy but enlightening stuff about turning forty, read the chapter called Regrets. You might be surprised by the regret that is most prevalent among men and women.

If you just want to have fun and understand why the transistor radio is more important to us than television, read the chapter on the Beatles.

The Landmarks chapter takes a look at the impact of the Vietnam War, the reasons why some of us skipped the drug experimentation of the sixties, and the ways in which we reinvent our past as we approach middle age.

The Baby Boom will have intense personal interest for people between the ages of thirty-five and forty-five but will also provide penetrating insight for anyone attempting to make sense of Baby Boomers, the sixties, and the process of growing up while staying young. So, whether you are curious, frightened, confused, cavalier, or simply interested in making the rest of your life better and more fun, there's something for you in *The Baby Boom*.

CHAPTER ONE

Confessions of a Forty-Year-Old

I Was So Much Older Then, I'm Younger Than That Now

This book makes sense of the Baby Boom generation as it reaches forty. This enormous "Big Generation," born between 1946 and 1966, grew up on rock and roll, challenged the social hierarchy of the nation, and turned youth into a potent force for change. At different times, Baby Boomers have been labeled juvenile delinquents, hippies, yuppies, or, simply, Boomers. In each of our phases, we have challenged the status quo — with rock and roll, drug experimentation, social protest, or status-driven conspicuous consumption; in short, we have presented a puzzle for those who have tried to understand us.

As we grew up, we believed our strength was our youth: Our generational slogan was "Never trust anyone over thirty," and we meant it. But, like it or not (and many of us don't like it), we are now turning forty. In each year between 1993 and 1998, more than four million Americans will turn forty.

However, as we pass through forty, we are not behaving the way "middle-aged" people are supposed to behave. We haven't given up rock music in favor of "easy listening" music. We still feel young and think of ourselves as young. We have continued our bold experiment in living.

In the not-too-distant past, forty was considered the start of "middle age," with its connotation of decreasing vitality, sexuality, and activity. Today, most of our generation knows that forty offers a second chance at life, an opportunity to apply everything we have learned to all the things we would still like to do. For some of us, though, forty is frightening because it suggests lost opportunity and the end of youth.

This book allows you to compare your experience with that of other Baby Boomers. It is based on the findings of the largest survey of Baby Boomers at forty ever published — findings that help us make sense of our generation and that explain why we are likely to continue to confound those who expect us to "grow old" in our attitudes and behavior.

You may be surprised to learn that, at forty, we are enjoying sex more. You may not be surprised to learn that we are having it less frequently than we did ten years ago. It may puzzle you that although we are becoming more religious, we are not attending religious services as often as we once did. On a lighter note, you might be interested to know that the Beatles are our all-time favorite band, with Elvis and the Rolling Stones coming in a strong second.

Throughout this book, I have woven in my own life experience as a sometimes typical and sometimes atypical Baby Boomer. I grew up at the leading edge of the Baby Boom. I never trusted anyone over thirty. I experimented alongside millions of others of our generation. I came face to face with the reality of aging in the course of a midlife crisis in my thirties. The idea of growing old didn't sit well with me, so I tried to understand what I could do about it. As I began to figure things out, I realized that the members of my generation shared many of the same formative experiences. So I decided to ask them how they felt about forty by conducting a massive research study.

The results startled and inspired me. At last, I could compare myself with the rest of my generation to see how I was doing, to learn where I fit in, and to explore what I could do about turning forty.

Armed with the research findings, my experience as a trend analyst, and my own personal story, I wrote this book to try to make sense of our generation at forty.

Crossroads

To be honest,I have mixed feelings about forty.

I love forty because I have finally learned enough about life to make sense of its broad outlines. I have more confidence than I did at twenty and a better sense of how to live the life I want. I know that the next forty years will be much better than the first forty.

I am uncomfortable with forty because I still haven't shaken the youth myth that I share with my generation, the Baby Boom — the "Big Generation." My gray hairs don't seem to belong. Where are the Beach Boys? Where is Endless Summer? Why do we have to age at all?

It's a monumental tug of war: I want the energy, enthusiasm, limitless optimism, and the body of twenty, and the wisdom, confidence, experience, and the mind of forty.

Like most of us, I arrived at forty the hard way, learning through trial and error, pain and pleasure. Along the way, I hurt people and I got hurt. I made bad mistakes but tried to learn from them.

Most important for me personally: I am more tolerant and patient than I was at twenty, but I still have a long way to go.

Of course, there's a nagging sense of the unfairness of it all, lodged at the back of the mind, that says, "If only I had known all this twenty years ago, imagine what life might have been like." Mistakes might have been avoided; opportunities might have been embraced. But no amount of regret can change the past. Letting go of regret is the first step to getting the most out of forty.

My mind, spirit, and soul feel good about my age. After all, minds, spirits, and souls benefit from experience and the time and opportunity to reflect. My body, however, isn't so sure that forty is such a great thing.

Gravity is playing a cruel game with me: my weight keeps trying to settle close to the belly button. And where did all those wrinkles in my forehead and around my eyes come from? When it comes to the body, forty tends to sneak up bit by bit, until suddenly we realize things have changed.

For most of us, the first shock of change is physical. We get overdrawn at the energy bank. One day, when we try to get up after a night of overindulgence, we find we have lost our bounce-back. At first, we ignore it, but then, after it happens a few more times, we begin to realize something really is changing in our life.

This physical change often triggers a search for answers about what is happening and why. It accelerates a lot of soul searching and self-questioning that begins around the mid-thirties. Like most of us, as my body changed and the energy bank drained, I looked for guidebooks and maps to give me explanations and some idea of what lay ahead.

Where Do I Go from Here?

The first thing I grabbed was Gail Sheehy's landmark book *Passages*. Quickly, I thumbed to Chapter 17, "Setting Off on the Midlife Passage." It helped a bit by showing me I was not alone. But knowing I was part of a large demographic tour group didn't give me a foundation for the faith I needed that this threatening change could be transformed into something positive.

I hit the bookstores and libraries at full speed. During the next few years, I read hundreds of magazine articles and books, ranging from *Esquire*'s "The Body at 40" to *The Macrobiotic Diet*. I learned about vitamins, hair loss, and aging. I thought about calcium and even joined a health club for a year. But as I pumped away on the stationary bicycle, reading a business magazine and watching the news on the club TV, I realized that something was still missing. My body was straining, but it wasn't in sync with my mind.

Suddenly, with the proverbial blinding flash, I realized that the issue was much more than graying hair, a growing stomach, and a drop in resiliency. I realized that the survival issue at forty is the integration of mind and body so that they operate as a unit rather than as Dodge City gunfighters trying to get the drop on each other.

There I was, supposedly helping my body on the bike, while my mind was churning through a business magazine and scanning the TV news to stay up on the latest corporate takeover. I wasn't paying any real attention to my body at all. I was just going through the motions!

As I sat there, frustrated over this realization, I suddenly heard Mick Jagger singing "You can't always get what you want, but if you try some time, you just might find, you get what you need." Some people get a religious experience. I got the Rolling Stones. But I still had to find out what I needed.

Now, I'm not the type to be "born again." I am innately suspicious of miracle cures. But I do have an open mind. I'm willing to look at anything from a different viewpoint and to try it, if it makes sense.

I began the journey through forty with what I thought was an open mind. But I'd barely set out when I came face to face with so much of my own resistance that it astonished me.

My Generation

While I was learning about myself, I kept running into other forty-year-olds who were going through the same process. We were all trying to make something positive from the fact we were growing older. Everywhere we looked, we found outdated information about forty.

There were so many idiotic "conventional" wisdoms that it stopped being funny. When these old-fashioned ideas were added up, they suggested that forty-year-olds were really old. That the best part of life was gone, including good sex, the chance to begin a new career, and even the possibility of finding the right life partner if your current spouse was all wrong for you. The ideas were not only outmoded, they were outrageous.

It struck me that the people trying to explain me and my generation were the same people who once told us that we would eventually stop listening to the Rolling Stones and begin listening to Mantovani. They told us that we would eventually come to our senses and stop experimenting with jobs, education, and personal growth — that we would put up with all the crap they put up with. Most important, they suggested that life was already fixed and set at forty, that there was no point in trying to make something with the remainder of life. I know they didn't understand my generation.

Members of the Baby Boom have confounded the pundits since we came into the world. We defied the "conventional" wisdoms at every step by latching onto rock' n' roll, challenging the educational system, experimenting with drugs, questioning the notion of marriage, and even putting off childbearing until as late as age forty.

We baffled the business world by pledging our loyalty not to a corporation but to an interesting job. In our teens and twenties, we frightened the nation with civil rights and Vietnam protests. It appeared as though we were unpatriotic. In reality, we were conducting a massive uncontrolled experiment against the status quo. In our thirties, we even experimented with consumer loyalties. At one point, our experimentation led to a huge increase in the sales of Japanese products, especially electronic products and cars. Today, we tend to experiment with American-made products. At forty, our focus on financial security has taken us into the investment market in unprecedented numbers, looking for better financial gains through stocks, bonds, and real estate.

As I reflected on my own growth and change, I realized that our Big Generation has unique values that we will use to shape society as we age. Conventional wisdom was of no use to us. We needed a new wisdom for our generation.

The more I thought about it, the more I looked for information, only to discover that almost everyone writing about the subject was relying on secondary sources. Sociologists were reading other sociologists, who were reading psychiatrists, who were reading historians, who were reading psychologists. There was too much guesswork and not enough fact.

And so, my journey at forty took a surprising turn. I decided to ask other forty-year-olds about their experiences. Specifically, I wanted to know how they felt at age forty about everything from their sex life to their regrets. By comparing myself to them, I could make more sense of aging. More important, it would establish important clues about the future, about where we are going and what we can expect to find when we get there.

Gathering the Facts

By profession and training, I am research oriented. For more than twenty years I have conducted and analyzed research for clients in fields ranging from advertising to media, from private schools to insurance companies. I have done research for CBS News, NBC, and MTV. I have researched everything from brand preference in bicycles to the way listeners respond to recording artists such as Herb Alpert and Bryan Adams. Working with my research partner, David Oakes, I have investigated everything from the desire for more "naughty" movies on pay TV to the political preferences of Baby Boomers. Through a network of contacts with other researchers, we have developed a broad understanding of the inner mechanisms of human behavior.

The more I worked with research, the more I noticed that people are fascinated by statistics. After all, who can avoid a peek at the latest poll, whether its subject is politics or the sex life of small-town America?

That's when the light bulb went on: I decided to conduct a massive research study of Baby Boomers between the ages of thirty-eight and forty-two, asking specifically about the experience of turning forty. This tight research focus would provide solid facts about our generation, facts that would help us understand ourselves better.

Keeping Score of One Another

My friend John McGhan triggered the process. As he approached his fortieth birthday, he said to me: "I'm turning forty next year. Where do I check in? How do I find out how I'm doing compared to other forty-year-olds? Am I fatter? Thinner? Making more money or less?"

His questions weren't surprising. As a generation, we have been shadowed by yardsticks and benchmarks since we were born.

By the millions, our parents read Dr. Spock to make sure that we weren't too short, too tall, too aggressive, or too docile. We began with a baby scorecard.

All through school, scorecards dogged us. Old-fashioned report cards gave way to such terms as "overachiever" and "underachiever." It didn't matter what we did as individuals; we were always being compared to someone or something else.

By the 1980s, public opinion polling had reached the point where we were all being compared to one another across so many different dimensions that we began to believe that the only thing that matters is other people's opinions.

It went so far that a popular TV game show called "Family Feud" prospered for years as the first quiz show with no factually correct answers! Instead, the answers were based on what 100 people *thought* the answers should be. "Family Feud" was a sign that scorecards based on someone else's opinion ruled the land.

With "Family Feud" in mind, I decided to poll my generation's studio audience — those between the ages of thirty-eight and forty-two — to find out what they thought about turning forty.

In this massive survey of more than one thousand people, questions ranged from how much we are enjoying sex at forty to our biggest regret. The survey probed the importance of the birth control pill, the Beatles, and the Vietnam War. It asked about physical fitness, diet, and even religion at forty.

The study covered a cross section of Americans, from residents of small towns to those of big cities, from people with grade-school educations to those with postgraduate degrees, from low-income earners to millionaires.

Turning Forty

When the results came in, they cast a bright searchlight on our generation at forty. In some areas, we are behaving according to the conventional wisdom. But, in most, we are not. We are a unique generation.

According to convention, as we get older and a little bit closer to death, we are likely to become more religious. According to a cross section of forty-year-olds, this is true.

According to convention, our interest in and enjoyment of sex go down in midlife. The survey results say "not so." We may be having sex less often, but we are enjoying it more.

The more I looked at the research, the more convictions were overturned.

Most Baby Boomer observers equate the Baby Boom with the Beatles. The research turns this assumption on its head. Close to a third of all Baby Boomers think of the Beatles as a negative experience and not as the musical gurus to a generation. They were most popular among college-educated Boomers who make more than $30,000 a year

There were more surprises about the importance of John Kennedy's death, and especially about Martin Luther King. When it came to the subject of regrets, there were insights and surprises. The insight came with the realization that biggest regret of most forty-year-old Baby Boomers is a failed relationship. The revelation came with those who said their biggest regret was getting too much education. Then there were women who regretted marrying too early and having children too early, counterpointed against those who wish they hadn't waited so long and regret that now they don't have a chance. The surprises continued.

I was surprised by the fact that nearly 20 percent of our generation have very poor or nonexistent pension plans and health coverage. I was titillated by the fact that more than 65 percent of us have had sex within the last week but amazed that 26 percent of single, unattached Baby Boomers at forty haven't had sex for more than a year.

By reflecting on the results of this unique survey, it's possible to capture the essence of the Baby Boom at forty somewhere between the statistical parlor game and the blunt facts.

> Forty is a very tangible signpost. People tell you you're supposed to feel bad and that when you're forty you're supposed to be something. Your frame of reference is forty-year-olds ten years ago.
>
> So, I wasn't excited about turning forty because I've cherished youth and freedom and having young attitudes, and forty seemed counter to that. The pleasant discovery is that it's not necessarily so.
>
> Instead, I'm young, confident, and in control of my physical senses. I'm still strong, I can run, and I know a lot more than I used to. It's so much better than I ever imagined it would be when I was twenty or thirty. Now, when I look ahead to sixty, that'll be a trip!
> *Jeremy, newspaper columnist*

Why This Book?

This book would not have been written forty years ago because, at that time, when you were forty it was too late.

It was too late to change your job, your family, or your life. Life expectancy was shorter, the work environment more rigid, and society less tolerant. Understanding forty wasn't worth the effort.

Today, we have an enviable range of choices for our lives and what to do with them. We are in charge. We can do something about our personal futures. We can do something good for each other.

For the first time in history, forty-year-olds anywhere can communicate *instantly* with other forty-year-olds. It's easy: Fax, phone, video, or face to face. This communication gives us the opportunity to understand one another better. We can explore in more depth and detail. We can compare notes. We can share hopes and fears.

As an optimist, I am encouraged by our possibilities and by the open communications available for exploring them together. Therefore, this book is optimistic. It views forty as the age at which we finally know enough to make sense of our own lives and have the confidence to do something about them.

In many ways, this book is a travelogue through forty, with stops at important places along the way. At each stop, there are sights to see and things to learn, for example, about sex, regret, health, and family.

As I assembled this travelogue, I kept three levels of the journey in mind: my personal experience; that of my generation as a whole; and, on a broader scale, that of an aging society. In many ways, my personal experience mimics that of my generation: I was raised on rock and roll, sought education after high school, lived with someone before marriage, and supported racial and gender equality. In other ways, my experience differs from that of my generation: I pursued a Ph.D., which kept me in school longer, and I put off having a child until I was over forty. I have drawn on both my similarities and differences to illuminate the explanation of our generation at forty.

The Baby Boom journey is the focus of this book. It is a journey of experimentation, apparent self-centeredness, and a commitment to staying young.

The third level focuses on an aging society. By our sheer numbers, we are increasing the average age of the population. Just as we crowded the schools, the job markets, and the housing market, we will crowd the systems designed to deal with an aging society — in particular, the health-care and the pension systems. The Baby Boom will be the core of this aging society. Understanding us will provide insight into ways of coping with the changes we will bring.

Will we confound our parents and all the armchair sociologists by turning our society into the Utopia we envisioned during the sixties? Will many of us end up living in old-age communes because we never had the children who might have taken care of us? Will the rest of our lives be rich and fulfilling? This survey provides a basis for the answers to these questions.

No matter where your interest in forty springs from, this book has something for you. If it's your birthday, it will make you feel better. If you're over forty, it will help you sort out the odds and ends that may have been unclear on your fortieth birthday. And if you are looking forward to forty with some unease, this book might make you want to hurry up and get there.

CHAPTER TWO

Landmarks

There Are Places I Remember

If aging is a lifelong journey, then landmarks are signposts along the way.

Some landmarks are so obvious that they hit us like a two-by-four. The death of a parent is a two-by-four. John Kennedy's death was a two-by-four. The Beatles were a two-by-four.

Others are complicated, changing, spread over a long period of time. They become clear only through the perspective of time. The Vietnam War was an important, evolving landmark.

Landmarks are important to us for two reasons. First, they give us an immediate jolt, a reorientation toward our world. They force us to reassess our lives very quickly. When we are hit at blinding speed by a sudden death, the outbreak of war, or a natural catastrophe, we ask ourselves what is really important to us, where our priorities lie, and what we should change in our lives.

After the immediate jolt, a landmark is filed away until we are ready to use it for its second big value. Landmarks lodge in our psyche, and we prod them out from time to time when we are trying to make sense of a difficult point in our life. They function like a navigational star or a highway signpost to give us direction. By looking back to landmarks, we get a true sense of perspective.

For example, if we feel we're not getting as far ahead in our careers as we should, we might look back to a landmark promotion ten years ago so that we can figure out how far we have really come.

Now that we are into the 1990s, we can look back on the landmarks of the 1960s and 1970s and put them into clear perspective. What did we learn? Were times really better then? Have we lost something along the way?

As a generation, we share some binding landmarks: John Kennedy's death, the Vietnam War, the Beatles, and psychedelic drugs. They differ from the landmarks that our parents' generation shared, and in this way they connect us to a distinct collective history.

> It's funny when you talk about landmarks. I feel
> like I have so many — from the first time I got laid
> to the time I finally made the basketball team. But
> no matter how much I think about those personal
> things, I'm more likely to think back to Vietnam,
> trying to get out of the draft, and, obviously, the
> death of John Kennedy.
>   Oh sure, the personal stuff matters — buying
> the first house, my first child.
> *Bo, regional sales manager*

Of course, we all have personal landmarks, including the death of a parent, an important event at school, a job, or the loss of our virginity. But, on the whole, these events are too personal to bind us together as a collective. However, these personal landmarks have a lot in common with our generational markers; that is, we treat them differently than our parents did, and this makes us unique.

Our parents shared two distinct, appalling landmarks — the Great Depression and the Second World War. Their memories and subsequent life patterns were shaped by economic catastrophe, savage warfare, and, in many cases, long periods of separation from friends and loved ones.

Like our parents, we suffered economic dislocation, but of a different form, thanks to inflation. We suffered the effects of two wars fought on remote battlefields, and in our living-rooms, on television. We saw women and blacks fight many battles in their social wars for a just place in society. Our landmarks reflect this.

Our landmarks also include previously taboo territory such as drug experimentation and increased levels of premarital sex.

It is not just that our landmarks were different from our parents'. We heard about them and communicated about them more rapidly because of technology.

Our generation witnessed an explosive growth in radio and television that created what we have come to know as a mass communications network. We saw and heard about landmarks as they were taking place. Mass electronic media came of age while we grew up. Then, as now, it developed a follow-the-leader mentality, looking for "the big story" and following it relentlessly. "Good film" got a lot of coverage. There was nothing like bullwhips in Alabama or pot-smoking hippies with headbands to bring out the camera crews. However, while newspapers, television, and magazines gave the impression they were covering the landmarks, communicating to the people, the real communication was taking place somewhere else.

For our generation, the real news was music. While our parents watched Walter Cronkite, we turned on the radio or the stereo and heard the news. It was all in the songs.

The songs told us all we had to know, whether we were going to San Francisco or leaving home. We sang along with "Eve of Destruction" and hummed "Ballad of the Green Berets." The poetry of our generation was in its songs. With music, we thought we could change the world.

Most of us can remember the songs that were popular when we found our first lover, spent that incredible weekend at the beach, tried marijuana, heard that someone we knew was killed in Vietnam, experienced our first marriage and our first divorce. We have songs for every occasion, and they are some of the biggest landmarks of all.

Yet, some events were so overpowering, so sudden in their impact, that all memory of music is obliterated. Only the stark image remains.

For most of us, the first volley in the series of shots that shattered our flowering idealism was the death of John Kennedy.

Abraham, Martin, and John

I had just finished writing my history exam. I knew I had mixed up a couple of generals, a few important dates, and a few minor battles. But the exam was over and I was relieved. It was a chance to go out and play.

Just as the exam ended, the presiding teacher said, "I have some terrible news for you. Another sort of history has taken place today. President Kennedy has been shot and he's dead."

Like my classmates, I was stunned. It wasn't possible. A young president with a young wife who had made me feel it was okay to be young was dead.

Like millions of us, I spent the weekend in front of the television set, watching the same scenes played over and over again, cementing in memory the first visual icons of a generation.

When John Kennedy was shot, we knew something was forever changed. We didn't know it, but it was the beginning of a long series of assassinations that would feed television's insatiable desire for image over story.

John Kennedy was the symbol of Camelot — of youth and of a new order. His death was very important to us and very negative, especially for women. Nearly 40 percent of women, compared with fewer than 30 percent of men, said his death was "extremely important." His death was an especially important landmark for forty-year-old blacks — more than 60 percent considered it "extremely important."

Although Martin Luther King's death wasn't as significant as John Kennedy's for our generation as a whole, it was even more important than Kennedy's for Baby Boom blacks. Fewer than 7 percent of whites said his death was important, compared with 80 percent of blacks. Unfortunately, it wasn't the last assassination to affect our generation.

If we fast-forward nearly twenty years, we face another cultural landmark — the assassination of John Lennon. Even though it wasn't a personally important landmark to most of us, it registered as a very negative event in the survey.

The death of John Lennon meant that the 1960s were finished forever. There would be no Beatles' reunion. There would be no chance for the aging Baby Boom to collectively re-experience the magic of their youth.

The shooting of John Lennon capped a decade of inflation, terrorism, and unprecedented levels of socioeconomic change. Therefore, it's not surprising that nearly 80 percent of all forty-year-olds felt negative about John Lennon's death. The more education you had, the more important his death turned out to be.

The cumulative impact of the assassination of John Kennedy, Robert Kennedy, Martin Luther King, and John Lennon has been enormous. It began a shift toward cynicism, anger, and despair. Ironically, it got us interested in news at a very early age.

> In 1963 I was a sophomore in high school in a journalism class. Over the speaker, the principal said something about Kennedy dying. It's funny, but it got me listening to the news. From then on, I really got into listening to the news.
>
> By the time Robert Kennedy died, I was such a skeptic I'd almost come to expect it. The same for Martin Luther King. And I never believed any of the stories about those guys being lone assassins. I still don't believe that.
>
> *George, radio newsman*

> It was a tremendous horror and loss of innocence to think that someone like John Kennedy, who held so much hope and who actually could be related to by kids my age, could be just callously cut down like that. And it was the first great vacuum created in my gut to think that the world was that evil and cruel. I didn't really feel that way again until John Lennon was shot.
>
> *Arthur, antique dealer*

As landmarks, assassination deaths plant two troubling seeds. The first seed says: Don't take a stand. Don't go against the grain or be different. If you do, someone will kill you. The second seed says: You have no control. The message is that no matter how much you plan your life or achieve success, you can be struck down by fate around age forty.

These seeds have taken root and put forth fruit. And a terrible fruit it is. We have abandoned the ideals we once had. We are afraid to take a stand, preferring to "let the other guy do it," and we are slowly being taken hostage by the forces of fear and fatalism.

If assassinations can have such a strong cumulative impact, it's no surprise that the Vietnam War tops the list of social landmarks for our generation. There's nothing like the thought of being killed in a foreign country, fighting a war you don't understand, to focus the mind's attention.

Don't Give a Damn, Not Going to Vietnam

Of all the topics I researched for this book, none generated longer, more passionate conversation than the Vietnam War. The memories were vivid and immediate as people spoke about an experience that terrified them, whether they had been in battle or anticipating the draft.

For those who escaped the draft, there was a guilty relief that they had been spared. For those who went to Vietnam and came back, there was anger and bitterness.

More than anything, it was the detail that was so telling. Those who escaped military service through subterfuge retold their stories with a mixture of pride and guilt, almost like a child who has devised a particularly cunning way of stealing candy from the store.

Those who served told their stories with a solemn, self-righteous anger.

The universal leveler was fear.

> The one thing I did not want to do was go in the war because all my roommates at college — I had four of them — had been in Vietnam and they were all fucked up beyond belief, and still are to this day. None of the four can hold down a regular job. All of them told me not to go.
>
> But when I got out of college the Vietnam War was still on and I had the bad luck to draw No. 68 in the lottery. Any number under 125 was sure to go.

They called me down for a draft physical, and I went out immediately and got counseling on how to get out of the draft.

I was considered borderline fat, so my counselor said, "I suggest you eat a pizza and drink a case of beer a day until you get to your draft physical." I was more than man enough to do the task.

The counselor also taught me to squash up my neck and how to shrink two inches off my height by using concentration and by lowering my head into my neck. So, I did it when I went to the physical.

Then, they sent me to the psychiatric evaluation. The guy next to me looked like Melvin Catsmilk, from high school — blond hair and horn-rimmed glasses — and he was explaining to the doctor about his heroin addiction. So, everyone was trying to get out. But I got on the scale and I was too fat and I was too short, but they had me go to my family doctor every six months for the next three years, and thanks to some judicious planning on my part I always weighed too much during that time and got out of the draft.

I tried to get out so hard because when I was in college everybody was coming back and anybody who had lived, who was lucky to live or get out unmaimed, got the G.I. bill. So, college was filled with friends who told me horror stories that made *Full Metal Jacket* or *Platoon* look like a cakewalk. No wonder I wanted to get out.
Mitch, banker

Over and over, those who escaped the draft talked about the fear and the dawning reality that it wasn't a television show or a movie in Vietnam. People were killed, maimed, and psychologically destroyed by a war that they didn't understand and weren't prepared for.

I was going to a military college in Georgia, and
one of my best friends there had a brother who
was in Vietnam. We got letters regularly and they
often included things like pongee sticks and all the
horrible goodies the Viet Cong were using out
there. And then people started dying, and a few of
the kids I had gone to school with were killed over
there. This left a lasting impression on me. I was
twenty or twenty-one and I didn't know whether I
was going to make it to twenty-three.
Barry, salvage diver

Why was Vietnam such an important landmark? After all, our parents
and grandparents had fought wars. What made this war different?

The biggest difference was that there was no clear moral imperative
for fighting the Vietnam War. Ostensibly, it was a war against commu-
nism, but the exact rationale for U.S. involvement was never clearly
identified and supported.

Also, the war was fought in an old-fashioned way. America had
gained independence two hundred years earlier by fighting an unorthodox war against orthodox British tactics. But, in Vietnam, the Americans
were outmaneuvered by the Viet Cong, who fought a jungle war using
unorthodox tactics.

Moral imperatives and unorthodox military strategies don't explain
enough. The real difference was that the Vietnam War was fought daily
on television. It was a battle of images without the smell of death and
blood, without the heat and humidity. It's no surprise that filmmakers
such as Francis Ford Coppola and Stanley Kubrick have focused on the
almost hallucinogenic qualities of a real war fought by real people,
flattened and sanitized onto a television screen.

I was sitting at this party about twenty years ago in
a conversation with an ex-Marine who had just
gotten back from Vietnam. He was very bitter and
very angry.

Suddenly, as we were talking, he opened up his
shirt, and he had these five bullet holes across his

torso, and he just kept yelling and yelling, "Audie
Murphy made me do this. Watching Audie Murphy movies made me stand up in the middle of a
fire fight, ruined my life and I am fucking crazy,
you know." And, suddenly, I felt very different. Not
like a totally flipped-out vet, but different.

And I got in my car and drove back to the air
force base and I saw the exit marked "30 miles an
hour" and I started to get really angry and really
depressed, and in a complete attempt to off myself
I just floored it, and by the time I hit the curb I
was probably doing 80 miles an hour and the car
left the pavement, flew right over the guardrail,
and went down the stupid embankment. Spun
around in the air but landed flat on its wheels. The
miracle was I was barely scratched.
John, producer

The Vietnam War was a landmark in two very different ways. First, it
marked unprecedented opposition on the part of American youth to a
war they were being asked to fight. Second, it unleashed imaginative creativity in lying and deceiving on a mass scale.

I went through exhaustive, very detailed analytical
and scientific ways to get out of the service. And I
don't feel guilty at all about it because I'm alive and
those people who died, no matter what they say,
died for shit. I decided I wasn't going to lend my
body and my life to a useless nightmare in Southeast Asia, and I beat the draft.

I approached it like a graduate school project in
marketing. Find out what the customer wants, in
this case the draft board who would exempt me,
and then find a way to give it to them.

I found a graduate student who was doing his
thesis on the draft and asked him to give me all the
malingering reports and said, I'm going to find out

what the fuck I need to do to get out of the draft.

After six months of research, I found my disease and then went to a doctor and began to convince him that I had it. I lost thirty pounds, I complained about irritable colitis. I was able to tell him I took four shits a day, and I was uptight with chronic neurosis and high blood pressure.

To top it off, I joined the navy reserve, and my doctor said, "There's no way you can go on active duty, you're in rough shape." The army examined me and let me go.

I was so happy I took the information on all the diseases I had studied, Xeroxed it, and gave it to a circle of friends of mine. Each one picked a disease, ranging from migraine headaches to obscure bowel disorders. They all got out. We're alive. We don't feel guilty about it.

Randy, radiologist

Men feared the war because they could be drafted and sent to die. They hated the war because it was wrapped in a government newspaper made of yesterday's lies. It created distrust in government among a whole generation, putting them at odds with their parents, who had trusted the government to save them from the Great Depression and to lead them in a war against Japan and Germany.

Women feared the war because they might lose loved ones. They hated the war because of its violence and its catalytic power to spawn lies.

The war became a focal point for the personal and political frustrations of the largest youth generation in history. Fueled by idealism, untempered by any real hardship, millions of us lashed out against a system that seemed to be going wrong.

It is so hard to talk about this because it comes flooding back in so many little pieces that kind of fit together.

I remember a letter from a boyfriend with pages

and pages of how incredibly beautiful Vietnam was and how he would like to take his R&R, and then in the next paragraph he wrote: "time to crawl back on my belly to the barracks. Write to you next week." And he had to crawl because there were snipers outside, so that twice a day he crawled back and forth with gunshots over his head.

Another fragment. I was so torn about the war. People I worked with were against draft dodgers and had a "love it or leave it" mentality. And yet my friends were in university, burning down buildings and getting arrested.

In Youngstown, Ohio, where I grew up, which was very close to Kent State, my girlfriend's sister was killed by the National Guard. That changed my feelings. That was when I began to say, "This is wrong. This is horrid. This must stop." And I realized my government was lying to me.

I hated the violence. I hated what was happening on campuses. The news was like watching Beirut today, with universities being burned and the National Guard overtaking a campus and pushing unarmed university students back with bayonets.

I was living in Detroit during the riots, and when I saw tanks coming down the John Lodge freeway, it could have been Vietnam. Seeing Detroit go up in flames shattered me.
Arlene, copywriter

Vietnam gets all the press. An unpopular war that fueled widespread student demonstrations makes great news. Bombing unarmed civilians and napalming children makes a compelling, if horrifying, story.

Yet, when the history of the twentieth century is written, Vietnam will be a footnote. A larger global landmark — a different kind of revolution — may merit a paragraph or two. That landmark our generation moved to, danced to, and even made love to: rock 'n' roll.

Rock 'n' Roll Music

Rock 'n' roll is the biggest landmark of our generation not because it made the world a better place to live, but because it symbolized freedom, because it brought blacks and whites closer through music, and because it heralded the technological entertainment age.

With our transistor radios glued to our ears, we imagined ourselves freed from all our troubles, singing or playing the guitar in front of a crowd.

In spite of our parents' frequent complaints about the "noise" we listened to, we realized that music was freedom. Music spoke our language.

Millions of us bought guitars, drum kits, or anything we could lay our hands on, and set out to become the next Rolling Stones or Beatles.

> I was a Goldwater supporter in 1964, and then two years later, by the end of high school, I was going to radical meetings, the lefty, druggy crowd. Through them I discovered more adventurous music and decided I should try to learn how to play this stuff. Then I got the "let's form a band" urge and it started.
>
> Our first band in a college dorm was called "Oedipus Rex and the Motherfuckers," which was as outrageous as you could get. Next, a friend called from San Jose and we went up there and formed a band called Savage Cabbage, lived in a communal arrangement, struggled for six months on no money, and finally realized we weren't going to make it.
>
> I was going to get married, needed a steady income, and it all went away.
>
> *Ken, rock journalist*

For everyone who started a band, there were thousands who just listened to the music. The Beatles, Rolling Stones, Doors, Led Zeppelin, Who, Jefferson Airplane, Bob Dylan, Simon and Garfunkel — a long list of astonishing musicians spoke to and for our generation, and for many of us, their music has endured.

In the midst of all the musical experimentation that marked the era, hundreds of bands came and went, with only a moment of glory. Peanut Butter Conspiracy, Moby Grape, and the Fugs left their shadow imprint and were gone.

Rock 'n' roll was revolutionary because it was a brand new form of music made possible by electronics. It was entwined with technological advance; steady increases in standard of living; and a huge, receptive audience of teenagers. It brought black music into the mainstream and exported an American style of music to Europe, which was then re-exported back to America.

Rock 'n' roll focused our generation's attention on the power of music — not simply as an entertainment vehicle, but as generational poetry that told us that the times were changing, that we were important, and that we could make a difference.

While television spoon-fed us the conventional pablum of "Father Knows Best" and "Ozzie and Harriet," music chronicled our real world, with powerful songs about love, death, anger, and despair.

To be sure, not all the lyrics we embraced were profoundly philosophical — "Who put the Bomp in the Bomp, Bomp, Bomp," for example — but on the whole, the music became a familiar soundtrack for our generation. Movies such as *The Big Chill* generated a collective gasp of recognition, less for the characters and plot than for the music. As Mick Jagger sang during the funeral scene, half the audience knew all the lyrics, felt profoundly moved, and were transported back in time.

The music was a landmark. It provides a point of reference to compare where we have been with where we are now. We will sing the songs in the old folks' home.

This huge musical experiment called Rock 'n' roll was intertwined with another, more troubling, experiment — the experiment with mind-altering drugs.

One Pill Makes You Smaller, The Other Makes You Tall

With hindsight, many forty-year-olds look back with anger on experimentation with drugs, especially LSD. Those who never tried drugs resent the fact that they were often badgered and made fun of for being "straight" and conservative. The few who ruined their lives through drug dependency wish they had never started. But, for millions of us, recreational drugs — especially marijuana — were a significant landmark.

> I think at the time everyone had to try marijuana.
> And looking back at it, I kind of wish that I could
> have missed all that. But everybody tried it out. It
> was just the thing to do. We gradually grew out of
> that as our kids got smart enough.
> *Betty, dental hygienist*

Marijuana is not a narcotic like heroin. It is not a stimulant like cocaine. Instead, it acts on the brain center associated with memory, creating mild distortions in time and space. It opens up auditory awareness.

To a very large extent, marijuana experimentation and musical innovation went hand in hand. While "turning on" with marijuana, millions of Baby Boomers lay on living-room floors or sprawled in beanbag chairs, eyes closed, listening to music. The drug altered expectations, perceptions, and judgment — in performers as well as listeners, encouraging musicians to "break the rules" and unleashing an explosion of technological and artistic growth.

On the technological side, manufacturers created stereo systems capable of reproducing everything from the beat of a hummingbird's wing to muddied layers of distortion on a bass guitar. Record producers worked to create sound fidelity and track complexity that took music beyond the concert hall and into the realm of the plastic arts.

Of course, there is something of the chicken-and-egg conundrum about marijuana and music. Did widespread drug use fuel the demand for more complex textured musical forms, or was it the other way around?

I think that widespread experimentation with marijuana created the demand for newness in sound simultaneously with the growth in supply. Coincidentally, most of us were between fourteen and twenty and in the process of experimenting with our musical tastes, trying to decide whether we liked progressive rock, folk, classical, or something else, when marijuana use became commonplace. Planted in that rich earth of experimentation is the rock music that still endures today.

Some who tried marijuana also tried mescaline and LSD, entering a hallucinogenic realm that was quickly converted into new forms of painting and art.

Regardless of one's moral position on drug use, it was an important landmark for our generation and provided us with additional impetus to see the world in a new way.

> These days, drugs are something that seems to have been around for a long time. At the time when we were doing them, it was sort of experimental, particularly with things like pot and mescaline. The biggest difference from today was it wasn't totally geared toward partying.
>
> We were trying to figure things out about ourselves and about the world, and we were kind of using pot that way. I don't think that exists much anymore.
>
> I love to smoke a joint and then dictate a draft. But the younger generation don't do that. They use it to get stoned and bang their heads.
>
> And that's the other important thing. Only some of us were tuned in. But there is a misconception among the younger generation today where they think that everyone was tuned into the '60s.
>
> They don't realize that we had our own preppies and sort of yuppies at that time too. There might even have been more of them, but no one paid attention. We got all the publicity.
> *Hans, TV writer*

In spite of our widespread acceptance of the drug culture, most of us gave psychedelic drugs a miss. More than 75 percent of us say they were "not at all important," and for more than 75 percent, they generate powerful negative feelings.

Only 10 percent of forty-year-olds surveyed were positive about psychedelic drugs, feeling they generated important personal and social change. They point to positive life changes made by some experimenters, including Richard Alpert, a friend of Timothy Leary, who changed his name to Ram Dass and has spent the remainder of his life helping the terminally ill, raising spiritual consciousness, and encouraging people to lead a good life.

But, on the whole, most forty-year-olds who experimented with drugs in the 1960s and 1970s have given it up in the 1990s.

> I have some friends in their sixties that smoke
> dope and people that are a little younger than I
> who are really into it. But most people my age can
> take it or leave it, and usually have stopped buying
> it.
> *Margot, high school teacher*

Even though most of us have given up drugs and many have become complacent about Rock 'n' roll, one of our significant landmarks is still evolving for us — the ongoing emancipation of women, which began with the sexual revolution.

Freedom

I remember the first time I had sex. It was sort of like the experience of jumping out of an airplane — exhilaration tempered by the knowledge that the parachute might not open. Too many of us had seen friends hurriedly married while Junior Walker and the All Stars played "Shotgun" in the background.

Back then, responsible men wore condoms, but even that method wasn't foolproof. So, every act of sex we engaged in was overshadowed by the conscious or unconscious awareness that it might lead to pregnancy and marriage. No wonder we kept asking whether we loved each other.

The birth control pill changed all that.

Almost overnight, fear of pregnancy was virtually eradicated. Finally, women were no longer trapped. They could enjoy sex without worrying about the consequences.

Whereas previously women kept a weather eye on boyfriends to see if they would make good husband-and-provider material in the unfortunate circumstance that pregnancy resulted from sex, with the birth control pill, women could choose men simply for fun, and they did. The tiny pill became a landmark stepping-stone to women's liberation. More than 70 percent of the women surveyed said that the Pill was personally positive.

Freed from fear of unwanted pregnancy, women began to explore such options as further education and careers. They didn't like what they saw — men systematically blocking them, consciously and unconsciously, from advancing.

After all, we had all been raised to see June Cleaver and Harriet Nelson as female role models, and men were slower off the mark in realizing something was lacking. The struggle to raise consciousness about women's issues, to figure out how to integrate into the mainstream, became known as the women's liberation movement. Like all revolutions, it gained the most attention through violence, although, most often, it was violence against the bra.

Interestingly, as many women as men were terrified by the prospect of freedom and change. They liked "Ozzie and Harriet" and "Leave It to Beaver" as much as men did, and cherished the notion of a world in which men did all the providing, and women all the nurturing. Yet, bit by bit, their consciousness changed.

> I was never a women's libber. I still like men opening doors and I was never into that liberation stuff until I saw so many inequitable situations.
>
> I was in a sales meeting where a female sales rep went up to one of the men, a vice president, and said, "How come you don't have any women in your region?" and he said, "The only way, in my opinion, a woman can sell is if she drives a van and has a waterbed in the back of it."
>
> There comes a day when all those things start adding up and you start thinking back and you ask yourself "How could I stand back and let all those people get away with those things?" So, slowly I've

changed, and now I've got a little button in my
office that says: "The best man for the job is a
woman."
Melanie, electronics sales

In the early days, as women were casting around for guidance in
weathering the storm, several key books opened the doors. They included Marilyn French's *The Women's Room*, Betty Friedan's *The Feminine Mys-
tique*, and Germaine Greer's breakthrough argument for feminism, *The
Female Eunuch*.

I was very conservative politically through the
1960s and the early '70s. As I get older, I'm more
concerned in social justice and taking care of those
who can't take care of themselves. This has come
about because of my experience as a woman and
the difficulties in dealing in a male world and the
barriers that were there for me.
  It began in my mid-thirties, after the birth of
my second son, when I was looking around to
make sense of changes I was going through. And a
book on the list of forbidden books by the
Catholic church, *The Women's Room* by Marilyn
French, changed my life. I knew that if I opened
the front cover my marriage would end, and when
I turned the page I started to get free.
Kim, layout designer

The landmarks in women's liberation were different from more obvious markers, such as the killing fields of Southeast Asia or the sudden
perceptual disorientation of psychedelic drugs. For women, the changes
were wrought in words, in the writings of such pioneers as Gloria
Steinem, who provided women with the help they needed to overcome
their lack of role models, the ferocious pressure exerted by male society,
and their own willingness to undercut each other.

Jane Fonda impressed me because she kind of

symbolizes the turning point for a feminist point of view when she went from *Barbarella*, where she was in bed with sexy Roger Vadim, and then married a radical, political, unattractive, un-Hollywood type of man and did what she believes in. Germaine Greer provided a turning point with *The Female Eunuch*. That was stuff I never would have been able to get into unless someone led the way. She helped me overcome my own fear of being a woman.

When I was looking for work, I would always say "I'm not a feminist" in order to get the job because I wanted the work and I thought it didn't matter if I said that because I'll still be able to get my point of view across anyway. But it was a terrible compromise. It was the kind of sacrifice that erodes you.

Perhaps the best thing about women's liberation is that women are finally telling each other the truth. We used to lie about how good our relationships were. We used to lie about how happy we were. It was a competition, who could pretend to be the happiest, when we'd go out.

Now we tell the truth. Yes, he is a total shithead. No, he has never gone down on me. Yes, I didn't have an orgasm till I was thirty-five. We are finally talking about it. There is strength in that.

I am more politicized than ever before. I was totally apolitical before. I am more political now. And I am a feminist.

Frances, swimming coach

Women's liberation rode a wave of social changes, including later marriages, more frequent divorces, and a shift in the age of childbearing. Although we appeared to be a generation of late bloomers, we were actually doing multiple dress rehearsals for maturity. As a result, we are integrating a remarkable range of changes healthily into our life at forty.

Yet, no matter how mature we are, we keep thinking back to high school and wondering what happened to all our friends.

The High School Reunion

Most of us shared a very similar high school experience. We crowded the classrooms. We expanded our minds and questioned our teachers. We were taught roughly the same subjects in roughly the same way. We discovered "necking" and "petting." We developed confidence or insecurity as a result of our experiences there. Twenty years later, we look back on high school as a landmark in growing up.

Like it or not (and most of us didn't like it) high school was the last time we were sealed in a peer-group pressure cooker from which there was no escape.

Manipulated by roller-coaster hormones, searching for an identity independent of our parents', and trying to figure out the meaning of life, we gasped a collective sigh of relief when we finally graduated. High school graduation was a big deal. It opened up a world of possibilities, freed us from the class bully, and told the world we were adults. Yet, it is difficult to leave high school behind.

High school was a place for so many firsts: sex, real learning, more competitive sports, fashion pressure, and a wider range of outlooks than we had ever seen before.

High school was our last self-contained world. A cool haircut was more important than an A in geography. Sudden development of breasts turned a girl from a wallflower into Miss Popularity. Teachers had a special power to encourage or crush our curiosity. And a few dollars meant the difference between being able to join in and being left out.

For most of us, a high school reunion can help purge us of the demons that haunted us and focus us on the fact that we are forty and free to choose a life and live it.

> I am much better off than the other people I went
> to school with. And I know that from just having
> been to my twentieth reunion.
> I went to a really working-class high school,

and they have ended up as firemen and Eaton Park Restaurant waitresses. I am the only one with an advanced degree.

To me it was a real validation to go back and say "people really liked me after all." All those adolescent fears and insecurities are wiped away. I was actually surprised that people were glad to see me. I was glad to see them. It was really fun. I didn't want to spend a whole lot of time with them, but I wanted to see everyone and go around to everybody and get a slice of their life.

Shana, professor

Down Close and Personal

Our generation's relation to landmarks is unique because we shared so many of them through mass communication, specifically, radio and television. For us, everything happened at the same time. We didn't learn about it months or years later and then have to try to put it into perspective within our own lives.

We all watched a man land on the moon at exactly the same moment. The Cuban missile crisis, Nixon's resignation, the Olympic boycott, the first Beatles single, and many other events were instantly and universally shared. Our landmarks are attached to moments in time that we share consciously and unconsciously.

As our generation ages, we will share new landmarks, such as the war with Iraq or the AIDS epidemic. Our parents will die. We will lose friends. These sad but necessary reminders of our own mortality will be weighed with the landmarks we have already lived through.

There is one landmark that will remain important to us for years to come. It permeates our current life and sets the stage for the next half.

It is our work and the money that goes with it.

Money and Work

Get a Job

I must have been crazy. For nearly twenty years, I figured I could avoid getting a "real" job. Avoid — as if a job were a form of socially sanctioned prison sentence with hard labor.

Avoid getting a job. The phrase smacks of welfare bums, laziness, and a near anarchistic irresponsibility. What in the world was I thinking?

Although I didn't know it at the time, I was behaving true to form as a Baby Boomer. I was experimenting with jobs. And it was all a result of too much change. The explanation is simple.

Like all of us, I grew up during a period of nonstop social and technological change. Every year brought an innovation in technology, although the cumulative scope of the technological revolution didn't seem obvious at the time because we took change and progress for granted. When the first satellite, Sputnik, flew through the night sky, people ran to their backyards to see this miracle. A few years later, the launching of a satellite was no big deal. Other technological breakthroughs, such as the transistor, the birth control pill, color TV, and the computer, have each generated intense interest for a short period of time and then faded into the scientific background of our lives. Almost as

33

soon as one technological miracle is in place, we take it for granted and watch the next one come by.

Marching in lockstep with technological miracles were social revolutions that were equally far-reaching. Civil rights marches, integration, the Vietnam War, OPEC, women's liberation, and dramatic changes in family structures were part of our everyday life as we grew up.

Their sheer numbers made changes a constant in our lives. For example, the body of scientific knowledge has doubled every ten years since we were born! On the social side, phrases unknown to our parents became our generation's watchwords: civil rights, women's liberation, ecology, and so on.

Unconsciously, I, and millions of other Boomers, developed an important perspective on the world: In this environment of nonstop change, the old ways of doing things weren't working anymore. Our parents' methods for dealing with the world were inadequate in the midst of all this upheaval.

For saving money, our parents were punished by inflation. For believing in their government, they were given war and corruption. Their belief in the permanence of marriage was rewarded with divorce, and their job loyalty with plant closings. It didn't take long for me to realize I would have to try different approaches to cope.

Like millions of us, I became an experimenter. Unconsciously, we decided that if the old ways of doing things didn't work, we would experiment with new ones. And we embarked on an unprecedented period of experimentation in everything from jobs to lifestyles. Instead of getting married, we moved in together. We experimented with drugs, alternative methods of schooling, different kinds of jobs, and new forms of music and entertainment.

For a long time, I experimented with the idea of making a living without keeping a "regular" job. That is not to say I rejected work. After all, I had run my own business at age seven. Rather, I rejected the old-fashioned, "the boss is the boss" workplace where the employee was valued for obedience rather than innovation.

As a kid, I ran a lemonade stand during the summer. One day, it dawned on me that selling it at three cents a glass to the kids on my block would never make me a rich man. So, I hired two kids to pull wagons of lemonade to construction sites and sell it for five cents a glass.

Business boomed. I split the profits with my partners and I got my first understanding of the marketplace.

Until age twelve, I was a child-labor entrepreneur, running lemonade stands, fish ponds, wagon pulls (two cents gets you pulled around the block on a wagon), and paper routes. I didn't actually deliver papers myself. Instead, I took over routes for kids on vacation and subcontracted them. It was the old-fashioned, tried-and-true form of business that had gone on since the beginning of civilization.

Then, around age twelve, everything changed. I gave up business, started studying hard in high school, and took occasional summer jobs in construction only if I really needed the money.

A small scholarship helped me through university. I liked school and it seemed that I was beating the system by avoiding a stifling work world — "The Gray Flannel Suit" of my parents' generation. I liked avoiding that even better.

Once I graduated, I jumped from job to job, taking work when I desperately needed money and quitting as soon as I had enough. It never occurred to me that I could find a job I liked and make a living as well. In that respect, I was carrying baggage from my parents' generation, a generation who were thankful for any work during the Depression, no matter how much they hated the job. Then, after the Second World War, they just wanted to enjoy life and provide for a family. Carrying their Depression-era thinking, they were happy to have a job and they didn't ask much about satisfaction.

We are different. We want a job that we like. We want to make good money. We want it all. We are the best-educated generation in history. We know that there is more to work than the choice between a factory and an office. New technology and an expanding global marketplace have created opportunities that our parents and guidance counselors never imagined.

When I was in high school, guidance counselors tried to persuade every boy that his future was either in a factory or one of four professions — lawyer, doctor, accountant, or engineer. For girls, the choices were more limited — housewife, nurse, teacher, stewardess, or waitress. A pretty grim scenario for anyone with imagination, artistic aspirations, or even the desire to have fun.

Luckily for us, technology changed everything. When I started college, computer science was an arcane field that attracted a few adventurous nerdy types. These days, many of them are drinking piña coladas on their hundred-foot yachts in the Caribbean, having sold shares in computer companies for millions. My guidance counselor never even thought of computers as a viable field. If the nerds had listened to the guidance counselor, the yachts would have remained an unfulfilled fantasy.

This incredible choice of jobs is one of the greatest things about age forty. More than half the jobs that exist today were unknown when we were in high school. Our opportunities are enormous. However, because the world is increasingly complicated, more jobs take place in some form of office environment. Also, we still carry some of our guidance counselor's baggage and like to think of ourselves as "professional."

When we are asked to describe what kind of job we have, more of us describe ourselves as "professionals" than as belonging to any other job category.

Who Are You?

We are professionals, skilled laborers, and business executive/owner/managers. At least, that's how more than 60 percent of men and nearly 40 percent of women surveyed describe themselves.

The definition of *professional* has broadened considerably. Where it was once used to refer only to doctors, lawyers, architects, and a small group of highly trained specialists, today its meaning has expanded to accommodate a highly sophisticated, technologically complex world. Today, there are computer experts who have more professional training than neurosurgeons. There are artists who are better skilled in the use of state-of-the-art design machines than many architects. It goes without saying that more of us work in offices than ever before because information management is supplanting manufacturing as the biggest creator of wealth. (Interestingly, office work is still disproportionately a female purview; 21 percent of women surveyed describe themselves as office workers, whereas only 2 percent of men do.)

Perhaps the most profound change in job categories between our generation and our parents' occurred in the field of housewife or homemaker. These days, one in five forty-year-olds describes herself this way. Four out of five don't! If we think for a moment about our mothers' and grandmothers' generations, we see that the change in this area amounts to a reversal. An overwhelming majority of women in previous generations would have described themselves as housewives.

During the 1970s, "housewife" got a bad name. Part of the criticism came from us, a Baby Boom coming of age, determined to change everything, to take the world by storm, and to have it our way. But another, subtle, but equally powerful, attack on the status of "housewife" was led by our own mothers. They saw too many friends suddenly divorced in their forties or fifties, left without skills to fend in the workplace, abandoned by their husbands, and cheated out of alimony and child support.

For more than a decade, the role of housewife was viewed with skepticism, and even a hint of fear. What woman in her right mind would stay home to raise children with no certainty that her husband would stay married to her? Instead, women focused on gaining a solid foothold on the ladder of economic security in an attempt to reduce their economic vulnerability.

Interestingly, in the 1990s, the role of housewife can suggest either a positive or a negative economic status. In most marriages, both partners have to work in order to make ends meet. If a woman can stay home and take care of the children, either the husband is very rich or the family is so poor that they can't afford daycare or sitters.

As a generation, we are starting to recognize that parenting is more than private schools, great daycare, and a roomful of "learning" toys. This recognition springs from one of the most important changes that our generation has experienced since the revolution of the 1960s — the increasing demand for a high quality of life. And it has its roots in our search for status.

Keeping Up with the Joneses

Our parents were status seekers. And so are we. It's a fact that is ingrained in societies, throughout the developed world and throughout history. One way or the other, we feel a compelling need to show where we stand in the social hierarchy. Some of us get status from German sports cars, Rolex watches, or a home in the right neighborhood. Others get it from exclusive memberships in clubs whose antecedents go back hundreds of years. For some, the need is so desperate that we seek status through the achievement of our children, often pushing them where they don't want to go so that we can bask in reflected glory.

> You know, this whole status thing is weird. During the 1960s, status was kind of anti-status. I mean, you had your blue jeans and a tee-shirt and you didn't need much more. Maybe you got status from how big your stereo speakers were, but even that was just so everybody could enjoy the sound.
>
> Then, during the 1980s, I kind of noticed that I wanted people to know I was doing okay so I figured I would buy a lady's Rolex, but when I saw the price I freaked out and bought one off a guy on the street for $30 which nobody could tell was fake.
>
> Does that make any sense?
> *Louise, chiropractor*

Louise's behavior makes perfect sense. It explains why our generation is doing what it does. It has confounded marketers, but it is very easy to understand.

Let's begin with the assumption that we all seek status. When we were growing up, we looked to our parents and noticed that status consisted of a new car every two years, a move to a bigger house on a bigger lot, a title for Dad at work, and, if possible, a tan during the winter. Status was steak for dinner every night, paid for by an ever-increasing income. It was all so simple.

While our parents were working, their "real" income went up approximately 5 percent a year. That means that every year, after allowing for inflation, they had 5 percent more money than they had the year before. Houses were cheap, interest rates were low, corporate pension plans were good, and the world was expanding.

Inevitably, we expected the same for ourselves. Only, it didn't happen. Instead, our generation came on in a crowd: we flooded the school system, the workplace, and the housing market. We fought for job opportunities, and outbid each other for homes. During the 1970s, we got caught in inflation's slipstream, almost drunk on pay increases that sometimes topped 15 percent a year. Even though prices were going up, we spent like crazy to keep ahead.

By the early 1980s, we had a hangover. The recession put an end to inflation's party atmosphere. And something happened that we had never thought possible: Our "real" income went down, so that by the end of the decade, we could buy less than we could ten years earlier. It was a terrible shock.

During this period of transition from our parents' generation, we found out we couldn't keep up with their system of status. We couldn't buy a new car every two years or move to a larger house regularly. Many of us felt we were lucky to buy a house at all, especially in hot real estate markets, such as those of the West Coast or the Northeast.

So, without even noticing it, we invented status substitution.

Status substitution works like this. Instead of trading our cars every two years, we now keep them for an average of five years. Where is the status in that? It doesn't show until you open the door.

You drive up to a friend's in your five-year-old, slightly beat up Toyota. You throw open the door, and there it is, sitting on the dash — a $1,000 Alpine stereo system! Your friend thinks: "Wow, you're happening. An Alpine stereo!"

Or, you sit down with some friends for a beer and they all order Bud. You ask the waiter, "Do you have any obscure beers that cost more than five dollars from weird places that no one's ever heard of?" Your friends think, "Wow, a five-dollar beer from an obscure place. He's happening."

That shift from new and bigger to quality and cost is status substitution.

The Rolex craze of the 1980s was a particularly powerful form of status substitution. If we couldn't buy a $45,000 German car, we could buy a $3,000 watch and wear it on our wrist for the world to see. Friends would think, "Wow, a Rolex. That costs a lot. She's happening."

Now, when status substitution takes place, something funny happens to the marketplace. Items without status lose value. The middle drops out. If we couldn't see the status in an item, we weren't willing to pay for it and we bought generic products instead.

This fact confounded marketers all through the 1980s. They couldn't understand why Baby Boomers would go to the supermarket and buy no-name tomatoes to save fourteen cents, then turn around and buy imported Italian mushrooms that cost six times as much as domestic ones. It was status substitution. If we weren't going to get a raise at work, at least we could "treat" ourselves at home.

A Canadian supermarket chain capitalized on this brilliantly. The Loblaws chain introduced No-Name, low-priced products and caught a growing segment of the market. Then, they introduced an "upscale" line, called "President's Choice," of gourmet discount foods. Using a brilliant combination of direct marketing through a food newsletter as well as food/status television advertising, they captured a huge segment of the market, riding the status-substitution bandwagon.

Status substitution has gone so far that we check out the outer label on a person's running shoes to see how much he or she paid for them. Now, our children have picked it up, wearing the status names on sweat-shirts, shoes, and hats. And we have moved on to making the biggest status substitution of all — from quantity of life to quality of life. This has enormous implications.

We have finally accepted the fact that we are not going to get ahead financially as well as our parents did.

> That has been the hardest thing for me to take.
> Knowing that my parents have paid off their house, have a great pension, and are having a great time. Helga and I are barely making it, and I am out of sorts over this. But, lately, we've been talking at home about how maybe it's better that we do something about getting clean water and clean air than always worrying about how to get more money.
> *Jake, mailman*

If we aren't going to get a 5 percent raise every year, then we want clean air. If the corporate ladder is missing a few rungs, then we want time with our family. This is the status substitution that is driving the ecology movement. Politicians who ignore it will be run over. Of course, there will be a tug of war between the desire for jobs and the healthier world. But we are smart enough and determined enough to have a better life.

These days, status comes from having "biodegradable" garbage bags and recycling boxes. It is a profound, permanent change.

Loblaws, the innovative grocery chain, has already introduced a complete line of "green" products, which are environmentally safer. Not surprisingly, they're outperforming all sales expectations.

For most of us, the acknowledgment that money isn't everything will make us more, rather than less, picky about our jobs. We will look for daycare, event vacations, and better working conditions. Unlike our parents, we won't stay at jobs we hate with the expectation of a big pay-off farther up the line.

Take This Job, But Don't Shove It

There is so much talk about people who hate their jobs that we could be fooled into believing that none of us likes to go to work. Well, the good news at forty is that most of us like our jobs, and almost a quarter of us love our jobs. Not surprisingly, the more money we make, the more we like our job.

The suggestion is that, by age forty, we have experimented in the work force to find jobs that make us happy. And we aren't changing them as often as we used to.

If we believe TV and the movies, forty-year-olds change jobs as often as we change underwear. This view was particularly prevalent during the "go-go" 1980s, when it seemed everyone was changing jobs for a twenty-dollar raise and a cup of coffee. But the facts don't support this.

More than 40 percent of forty-year-olds surveyed have had the same employer for at least ten years. Another 20 percent have changed jobs only once.

It would appear, then, that we spent our twenties trying to get a clear idea of what interested us most, what provided the most security, and what gave us the best income. Then, most of us spent our thirties getting experience and increasing our cash.

Money, That's What I Want

No matter how much we talk about job satisfaction, we have to work to make money. And, for many of us, money has become more important now that we have reached forty — specifically, money for our old age, as a form of security.

> I've gone from being twenty and thinking money is not important and don't trust anyone over thirty and all that stuff, to thinking that money and financial security is very important to me.
> *Ginny, textile worker*

At forty, there is a nagging feeling that we just might live long enough to need money in our old age. It brings a specific focus to savings and accumulation.

> Lately, I've just noticed again this year that I have some kind of desire to accumulate more. To start making more money. Maybe to start trying to find outside projects that I could do without compromising my main job and bring in money from it.
> Very belatedly, there is a dawning sense of trying to establish my financial security. Both my wife and I have always been very heedless, spending up to the limits of our income, not saving much. Now, I think at some point you have to suddenly think about what's going to happen twenty years from now.
> *Lorne, fast food manager*

Lorne isn't alone in considering another job. Yet, when it comes right down to it, if we are having trouble making ends meet, we aren't holding down two jobs to do it.

Nearly 80 percent of us have only one job at a time. In part, this is a reflection of the fact that the majority of couples in their forties already have two incomes, obviating the need for any one of them to have two jobs. But there are a few really hard workers out there who hold two or more jobs. More than 10 percent of women and 6 percent of men surveyed have two or more jobs.

The big issue among our generation is not the number of jobs we hold but the kind of hours we work. There are so many new options, such as flex time, staggered hours, and split shifts, that accompany the radical reorganization of time in our workplaces.

When men and women both work but have to raise a family, the demands of school, shopping, job, personal time, and leisure build up a powerful head of steam.

Of those surveyed, more than 90 percent of men and more than 50 percent of women work full time; another 20 percent of women work part time. Work puts enormous pressures on all of us, creating a nation of time junkies who freak out if asked to stand in line for three minutes and who start to develop a nervous tick if a restaurant meal takes more than five minutes to arrive.

When my wife, Pat, and I were both working long hours, pursuing the cuddly dream of upward mobility we had observed in our parents, we were crazed to acquire money and were constantly pressured for time. Often, that meant that we would get home at 8:00 at night, exhausted and frustrated with long hours. We would both be too tired to cook dinner, so we would go out to a restaurant or order something in. A meal we could have cooked ourselves for $6 suddenly cost $25. And we wondered where our money went. There wasn't time to talk with each other, to relax, or even to get chores done.

That meant more dry cleaning, maid services, and other "luxuries" our parents never dreamed of. But, when we totalled up the cost, we realized that we were spending our money and our time and ending up in the same place. Like millions of forty-year-olds, we slowly developed an awareness that we were going to have to think ahead if all this work was going to pay off.

How Can I Be Sure?

This dawning awareness cast a long shadow. We began thinking about savings and investment. We began to consider cutting back on spending. In that, we were not alone.

> I think, pending the big 4-0, that I'm starting to
> think maybe I should cut back a little more. Be a
> little more conservative in terms of spending. And
> it's not like we've already spent a lot of money in
> our lives.
> *Gary, department store clerk*

Most of us try for some financial retooling around age forty. A little more focus on savings. Looking for more income from a different job. Looking at pension plans. Our focus shifts toward the future. Many of us make plans based on what we have now and what we might earn. However, for millions, there is a huge unknown factor in financial planning — inheritance from parents.

> I would be lying to myself and to this interview if I
> didn't say that the money I might inherit from my
> parents tempers my judgment in certain areas.
> My parents have a fair amount of money which
> I will inherit. Their house alone is worth five times
> more than they paid for it. Now, I'm not looking
> forward to them leaving it. I hope they will stick
> around for as long as they can. But there is a cer-
> tain comfort factor in knowing that it is there.
> *Alison, housewife*

Alison takes some comfort in the fact that her parents might not spend all their wealth before they die. She is one of the lucky ones. For many of us, when it comes to retirement and pensions, the news is not good. When asked to rate personal retirement/pension savings plans, most of those surveyed said they were inadequate.

Most shocking is the fact that 13 percent of men and 18 percent of women have no retirement/pension plan at all at age forty! This statistic is even more worrisome when we notice that 14 percent of college graduates have no retirement/pension plans. With only twenty-five years to go, theoretically, until retirement, we've got major financial rethinking to do. In fact, the only group who rated their pension plan as more than adequate were those making more than $50,000 a year, or those with postgraduate education.

This scares me. Even though there is an attempt to build up the Social Security fund, how will it cope with tens of millions of Boomers who turn sixty-five during a very short period of time? They will either have to tax us even more heavily as we get closer to retirement age or lower the pay-out.

In my late thirties, I suddenly realized that I had hardly any money in a pension plan. My friends parents' were retiring, and they seemed to have it made. At age sixty, they were golfing twice a week, planning a cruise, and spending winters in Florida. They had been lucky enough to live during a period of rapidly rising real estate prices, generous company pensions, and annual increases in real salary. I wondered what it would take for me to live comfortably, so I asked the chief actuary, the person who estimates odds, at a major insurance company what it would take for me to retire at age sixty-five on $2,000 a month, if I started saving at forty.

The answer was that a monthly contribution of $220 would have to be made, starting at age forty. This assumes contributions earn 8 percent to age sixty-five. It sounded good when I first heard it, but then I suddenly thought "What will $2,000 a month buy in twenty-five years?"

Yet, even when faced with these numbing statistics, I am superstitiously optimistic. Like so many of my generation, I think that somehow everything will work out, but I'm certainly going to give it a little help by trying to save more money every year.

Future focus is inherently optimistic. Most of us think we will figure out a way to take care of ourselves when we get older. After all, we've made it this far. And, as we look back to see where we've come from, we realize we wouldn't be comfortable living the way we used to.

Get Back

When things aren't going well, one of the comforting myths is the idea that we can adjust to hardship by going back to the way things used to be. However, on reflection, most of us realize that there is no going back, that we have adjusted our sights upward.

> I feel that my attitude toward money has changed
> and hasn't changed. I like to kid myself and say I

am still the same simple person that could live in a
hut on the beach or live off the land, but I know as
I've gotten older I'm not willing to compromise
about comfort the way I used to.

I don't think that I can every tolerate being
poor again. So, yes, I guess my attitude toward
money has changed. I hadn't really realized it. But
I guess I want money.

Ari, draftsman

The more we have, the more we get used to. Our expectations
change.

All of a sudden, you get some wealth built up in a
house and a standard of lifestyle that you like and
you begin to think — in 1971, it was no big deal.
All I needed was $100 a month to pay the rent,
buy some Fritos and a Big Mac, but now the $100
wouldn't last any time at all.

Sometimes you wish for the old H&R Block
days when they did your taxes in 30 minutes, you
paid $25 and you got a check back for a couple of
hundred dollars a few months later. What a simple
life!

Lee, radio manager

As we become comfortable, finally meeting our material needs, the
fear of going back is very real and very frightening.

I can't go back. I can't. A lot of people say they
could go back to living in a one-room bachelor
apartment and really roughing it and it wouldn't
matter to them. I have a big fear of that. I've
worked so hard to get this little piece of security
but sometimes it's like a snowflake in the desert. I
can't imagine going back. It bothers me every time
I look and see things deteriorating.

It scares me. This major thing about turning

forty hit me like a ton of bricks. I do not have one
red cent saved. That is a big problem.
Kareem, roofer

We are more concerned about money. We don't want to go back to
living the way we used to. We like cash. Yet, at forty, we are looking at
life for more than money. We want quality of life as well.

Are the Best Things in Life Free?

The best things in life are no longer free. But they are less expensive than
most of us think. Take health, for example.

Good health is one of the best things in life. Without it, we can't
enjoy much.

We contribute to our own good health by getting rid of bad habits,
eating properly, getting sufficient sleep, and doing all those things our
mothers told us to do. However, we can have even better health if we
can afford organic food, massage, healthy vacations, and a pollution-free
place to live. That is the paradox surrounding quality of life. It takes
some money to enjoy it fully.

When we work so hard to earn money, we can lose perspective on the
important things in life. It doesn't take a lot of money to have good
friends, a healthy body, or a positive mental outlook. It doesn't take
money to smell a rose or be uplifted by helping another person. There is
no price on happiness. Sometimes, it takes another person's tragedy to
shift our focus from money to friendship and what we really care about.

One of my customers is forty-one and he has a
brain tumor. He was jogging, passed out, and they
took him to the hospital. Now he's got a malignant
brain tumor and they can't do anything.

He's back at work and I see this man fading
every day, and he's forty-one years old. And all of a
sudden I thought, my God, I work so hard for
what I've got because I came from no money. What
happens if I die?

I mean I want to give it to somebody and if I

don't have a family, then I should give it to my sister or my brother, who need money. And then I
thought, I want to do some good. Maybe send
their kids to college or something. And I realized I
have to do a will.
Chris, stockbroker

Although the best things in life are free, it doesn't hurt to take out a little insurance. And, when it comes to health and medical insurance, most of us think we are adequately covered.

However, an unsettling number have poor coverage or none at all. Nearly one in ten surveyed say their coverage is very poor or they have no health and medical insurance. Close to 10 percent of women have none at all!

It is a scary thought that people can die in the richest country in the world because they can't afford a doctor. Or even worse, that they can lose everything they own — a house, their life savings, their car — to pay for medical care. Because, at age forty, most of us are fairly healthy. We haven't started to have the chronic and catastrophic problems that start to hit in the fifties, sixties, and especially the seventies. These include heart problems, arthritis, and cancer. If this sounds like depress-ing stuff, skip the next paragraph and everything will be fine. But, if you can handle the statistics, I asked the insurance company actuary about the odds on health costs in the future.

He gave me current annual costs and reminded me that these are the costs today, not in ten years' time. If we factor in the fact that health costs seem to increase by 10 to 12 percent a year, it means that these figures could double every seven years. To put that in perspective: for a man who is fifty today, medical costs would average approximately $1,700 a year; for a woman, more than $2,000. However, in ten years' time, when a forty-year-old man turns fifty, those costs could possibly be closer to $4,000 a year; for a woman, they would be pushing $5,000.

No wonder money is so much on our minds at forty.

Kids Are All Right

As if it isn't enough to worry about pensions and health insurance, kids complicate things even more. At forty, most of us have at least one kid. But, at least 14 million Baby Boomers will never have children. The reasons are simple and complicated. Simple reasons include infertility and nontraditional sexual orientation. The complicated reasons include a longer time in school, more time on the career track, and a feeling that we can cheat biology.

For most of my life, I never wanted to have children. My reasons weren't selfish ones. Rather, I was caught up in a combination of career orientation and global pessimism that conspired against me.

On the one hand, I felt it was unfair to bring children into a world that was overpopulated and actually on the verge of environmental catastrophe. If the rain forests keep burning, there may not be sufficient oxygen on the planet for today's children to breathe in fifty years' time. If the ozone hole keeps thinning, crops will fail, skin cancers will increase, and the world will be a terrible place. In part, I used my ecological negativity as an excuse not to have children.

In part, I was too focused on my career. Traveling out of town regularly, flying all over the place, working long hours and some weekends, I convinced myself that it would be unfair to put a child through this, so I shouldn't have one. But I could lie to myself for only so long.

Everything changed about five years ago when Brandon came into my life. My wife, Pat, had helped her brother, a single parent, raise Brandon since he was born. Although she was his aunt, she was as close to a real mother as he ever had. Before I knew it, Brandon was spending weekends, summer holidays, and Christmas holidays with us. I was thrust into instant fatherhood with a four-year-old boy.

Within a year, I loved him as if he were my own son and treated him accordingly. And the more time I spent with him, the more I realized that it takes a lot of money to raise a child. And, these days, there are so many more things that money can buy for them.

When I was a child, my family was poor. They tried hard to hide this fact from me, and we never went without food or clothes, but I was keenly aware of the fact that there wasn't a spare penny for luxuries. As a result, I have always managed my money well and been good at denying myself anything I don't really need. Good management isn't always fun, and sometimes I envy my friends who grew up in slightly more affluent families, comfortably getting into debt to have whatever they want, whenever they want it.

With kids, there are so many financial aspects to consider. There are day-to-day basics, such as food, clothing, haircuts, books, and toys. There is the future, which might include a car, travel, and a college education. Then, there is good parenting to think about. A child needs to learn the value of money, responsibility, and planning. This is one of the hardest things of all.

Most of us grew up while our parents' lives were constantly improving. Each year, they had more money, more opportunity, and more for us. Although many of today's forty-year-olds suffered hardship as children, on the whole we have had it better than most children in history. Therefore, it is particularly galling to find ourselves unable to provide the things we want for our children.

> The most frustrating thing to deal with is lack of money. Particularly for anybody that you talk to that has children. It is really hard. Because there is a built-in in the human being that you want the best for your kids and, when you can't do that, it is really frustrating.
>
> I grew up in a background of working people. The only books in my house when I grew up were an encyclopedia, and detective and sex paperbacks. But, then, I got out and went to college and now I try to provide my child the things I lacked as a kid. But it is frustrating that I can't get my daughter a new car to go to school with. To see how that affects her emotionally and affects her relationships with other people. And lately, I've had money trouble.
>
> So, now there are three of us living in a studio apartment and I'll wake up in the morning and say, "At forty, I can't do this much longer." What about my kid?
>
> *Joel, actor*

For most of us, the issue goes beyond survival to providing opportunity for children.

> I was pretty nonchalant about money when I was younger. I just never thought about it. If it was there, you spent it. If it wasn't, you didn't. Now, I would like to have enough to be comfortable. I mean, I am not into being rich or anything, but I would like to be able to educate my children.
> *Donna, geneticist*

Lack of money is stressful. Worrying about money causes stress. Even having a lot of money creates stress. It goes with the territory.

Stress, Stress, Stress

At forty, we have more opportunities than any generation in history. There are more types of jobs available, with more flexible hours and better pay. Unfortunately, the flexibility — irregular hours, uncertain deadlines, difficult timetables — creates physical and psychological stress. At the same time, the technical demands of modern jobs are much higher. We don't want to make mistakes.

All of this takes place in a changing social environment. Many men are still reluctant to accept the idea of their wives working. Caught up in a John Wayne time warp, they can't recognize a woman's need to expand her own horizons, keep her curiosity stimulated, and earn some extra money.

> I have a lot of stress right now.
> In my job, we have deadlines and problems that can pop up at times like 3:00 in the morning and I have to go in and fix it. It's computers, you know.
> I remember one time I was at a bar till 3:00 because my girlfriend came back from California and I hadn't seen her in years. We had just a great time, and then I got home and was called in to

work and I was out all night. You can imagine the
stress.

And then, there's my husband. He doesn't support me. He never did like me working, so it's been
hard. I tried to go back to school to a community
college, and he didn't back me up at all, so it was
very difficult. But it was something I wanted to do,
and I finally did get my degree. I think a woman
should be able to work if she wants to, as long as
everything else in the family is going well.
Diane, computer expert

Stress comes in all shapes and sizes. Our generation gets a dispropor-
tionate share of competitive stress because the economy has moved glob-
ally. Also, there are so many of us in the same age group that we are
competing with each other.

Being a salesman is a high-pressure job. The guy
that gets there first gets the sale. And my company,
even though it's a nice company, has got some per-
sonnel problems. They aren't very quick at taking
care of problems once you give them the situation,
and that's starting to bother me. It never got on my
nerves when I was younger, but now it's starting to
give me a little stress.
Clark, car salesman

With more women in the workplace, there are social stresses that
were minimal thirty years ago. Intelligent women work, marry, and get
pregnant. They want to spend time with their children, but they're worried about their job. It's a painful, tearing stress at forty.

I am the head of a department of fifty people. I
hire them, I fire them, I am responsible for all of
their clinical work, their teaching, their research.
And I report to the chairman of the department of
a major medical center.

> And it was really kind of stupid, but I was
> afraid to tell this guy I was going to have a baby. I
> didn't know what would happen. Would they fire
> me? Replace me? I was thinking this even though
> they had done a national survey and couldn't find
> anybody else to do my job. Isn't that crazy?
>
> As it turned out, it didn't faze him at all. I got
> paid maternity leave, and they were very kind. So,
> all my fears were unfounded. I guess they were
> irrational fears based on what I grew up on.
> *Joanne, medical researcher*

Old habits die hard, especially when it comes to one of the most frag-
ile items in the universe — the male ego. For all of our education,
awareness, and growth, men still have a problem with women who are
successful. It can affect a man, whether he is the boss or a boyfriend.

> This might sound unbelievable. But in my job
> right now, I'm one of the highest paid and the only
> female. I'm a top salesman. And for a year now, the
> man I work for has been trying to fire me because
> he doesn't want women in the company. He
> doesn't think I deserve to earn money that a man
> could have. And I'm afraid it's going to end up in
> court.
>
> And even weirder is what happens when I meet
> guys who make less than me and it starts to get a
> bit serious. It's like, all of a sudden, you meet
> someone that makes $30,000 and think, "This is a
> real nice person but if it works out it could be a
> real problem." Not with me as much as with the
> male ego. It's the biggest problem with me. Finding
> I meet men who make less money and they just
> can't handle it.
> *Marilyn, steel salesperson*

So, why do we put up with all this stress? Is it all worth it? Are we doing it so that we can have a better life than our parents did, just as they worked so hard to have a better life than their parents did?

How Am I Doing?

My parents told me to study hard in school. As new immigrants, they believed that education was the key that would unlock all doors. And in many ways, they were right.

Like the parents of so many of my friends, they made big sacrifices so that I could stay in school, get the education I needed, and get a head start in the world. They believed that my sister and I would have a better life than they had had and that it would, one day, have all been worth it.

I am one of the lucky ones. So far, I am doing better than my parents at this age. But, in a way, I am not so lucky. The house they bought for $17,000 in 1960 now sells for more than $200,000. A car comparable to the one my father paid $3,000 for in 1960 now sells for $18,000. Something has gone slightly wrong somewhere.

In his landmark book, *Great Expectations*, Landon Jones noted that the Baby Boom generation has lived its life with great expectations. We expected to be doing better than our parents, and better than the world at large, as we aged. But, how do we really feel at age forty about how far we've come and how far we've got to go?

I asked forty-year-olds this question: "Ten years ago, did you think you would be better or worse off at forty than you are now?"

More than 60 percent of respondents thought they would be better off than they are today! And among blacks, the number is even higher — more than three out of four. We have had a rude awakening. But, it is important to keep the expectations we have in perspective.

I asked forties another question: "Are you better or worse off than your parents when they were forty?" The answers are encouraging. Close to 70 percent of respondents felt they are better off than their own parents were at age forty. In other words, we've done better than our parents when they were forty, but we had such high expectations that we thought we would outdistance them by amazing margins. The next obvious question involves gazing into the crystal ball. If things haven't turned out as well for us at forty as we thought they would, how do we think they will turn out at fifty?

The best way to get a handle on this type of question is to ask how we are likely to do relative to other forty-year-olds over the next ten years. In other words, what does our future look like?

The answers are surprisingly realistic, and optimistic as well.

Slightly more than half of us think we will be better off than other fifty-year-olds ten years from now. This is an accurate estimate. After all, in any group of people, half will be better off and half will be worse off. That is simple statistics. We have become much more realistic in our outlook on the future. However, men, driven by the male ego, are less realistic than women.

Men are more optimistic and competitive than women. Close to six out of ten surveyed said they will be better off than their peers ten years from now. But we know that isn't possible. Only five out of ten can be better off than their peers.

So, 10 percent of the men turning forty are in for a rude surprise when they turn fifty.

These expectations are based on the fact that, right now, a forty-year-old man has an average annual household income of $41,000, and a forty-year-old woman an average annual household income of $39,000. The more education, the better the income.

A surprising majority of us own our own home — more than 80 percent — so things aren't that bad.

For some of us, no matter how well we do, there is a nagging fear that we don't really deserve it, that somehow we really aren't qualified for our success and that one day it will all blow up in our face. This phenomenon is called "the imposter syndrome."

The Great Pretender

The "imposter syndrome" results from the enormous changes in our world over the past twenty years. Millions of new jobs have been created that didn't exist when our parents conceived us. Many of them require skills that couldn't be learned in school. Suddenly, we are catapulted to an important position and paid a lot of money, and we aren't sure we are fully qualified.

The fear is natural. It is fear of the unknown. We have no framework, no model against which to judge our choices and decisions. It creates a very real, very frightening job stress.

> This is really weird. I have a job I like and I have
> succeeded in it. I make lots of money. But horror
> beyond this life, when are they going to catch on
> that I don't know what the fuck I'm doing?
> I have this inadequacy as I've been pushed up
> to this level, so I'm always trying to prove myself.
> And now I'm into it from a career standpoint so I
> work sixty, seventy hours a week and then take my
> work home with me. And I'm head of this big cor-
> poration, and even though I seem to be doing the
> right thing, I always get the feeling that they're
> going to find me out.
> *Tom, TV executive*

Twice in my life, I have almost been paralyzed by the "imposter syndrome." Each time, I've felt like Tom.

The most debilitating experience came about four years after I started
my own business. I had built up a long list of clients and was having
fairly good success. One day, faced with a very difficult competitive challenge for a hard-to-please customer, I suddenly lost my nerve. I began to
doubt my judgment, my competitive ability. For the first time in years, I
started to ask myself "What if I'm wrong?" and "How can I be so sure
that I am suggesting the right thing?" Over the next weeks, I tortured
myself with my inadequacy. Where was my professional training? What
right did I have to do this job? What if I am not as good as I think I am?

For a while, I felt as if the fear might overwhelm me, that I should
quit my job and just walk away. But, bit by bit, I got a grip on things. I
looked back on past successes, talked with my peers in the business, and
slowly convinced myself that I had the qualifications it takes.

Looking back on it, I realize that part of my problem stems from the
fact that our generation has grown up with two unique forces in our job
market. The first is our very wide range of highly specialized education;
the second is that millions of jobs that are available to us did not exist,
even conceptually, twenty years ago.

Our parents and our teachers convinced us that specialized training, ideally in a university or community college, was essential to competent job performance. If we didn't have the training, we couldn't do the job. Unfortunately, most of the jobs that became available emerged before the colleges could even create training for them. We had to learn as we went or be trained on the job. But this type of learning on the go was strongly against the current of what we were brought up to believe about formal education being mandatory for some jobs. It is no wonder that we have suffered periods of doubt, confusion, and blinding panic in the work-place. Ideally, as we get more comfortable dealing with change, we will feel less like imposters and more like creative survivors.

So, when it comes to money and jobs, we run the range of emotions from fear of unemployment to fear of exposure. Like it or not, most of us will have to work up until the day we retire, and it's clear that our focus will shift more toward the future as we age.

When I'm Sixty-four

Most of us don't hate our jobs. And we like them more if we make good money. But inevitably, we know one day we won't be working anymore — by choice, or because of mandatory retirement or disability. For most of us, work eventually ends and we face retirement.

Our parents sought retirement as the Holy Grail. It was a chance to kick back, free from the responsibilities of job or children, to bask in a combination of employer- and government-funded pensions. Work hard, keep your nose clean, be loyal, and the payoff comes at sixty-five.

At forty, we have doubts about this scenario. We have been through the massive "restructuring" of business during the 1980s that turned job security into a bad joke. We watch the nightly news where global competition makes headlines with predictable sameness. We watch "budget-minded" politicians cutting social security for the needy and bemoaning a deficit that they created and have no will to control.

Periodically, like an outbreak of plague, there is a rash of stories about the impending bankruptcy of Social Security, driven by a combination of an aging, longer-lived labor force and a government that can barely think beyond tomorrow let alone twenty years down the line.

When it comes to Social Security, we need to remember this important fact — when the program was conceived, the average life expectancy of a man was sixty-two. The government didn't have much to lose by promising pensions at sixty-five. These days, men live well into their seventies, and women even longer.

One in five women who are forty today will live to see their ninetieth birthday! Will Social Security be there?

> I've been saving like a maniac lately. My goal is
> $10,000 a year. I'm not counting on Social Security
> because I don't think it will be around when I
> retire, considering the amount of diminishing
> returns of the people paying in for the people that
> are withdrawing benefits. You'd have to be stupid
> to think you would get anything out of that.
> *Reg, radio sales*

We look for alternative forms of pensions, hoping that we can cover our bases. At times, the search locks us into jobs we don't like.

> I've been looking into a retirement plan, and they
> have some pretty good ones if you invest I think
> it's up to 10 percent. It's all tax deductible.
>   I was also considering leaving my job and going
> somewhere else because I am not happy with it.
> My friend told me that if I stayed till December I
> would be vested, which meant I could collect later,
> so I stayed, even though I don't like my work.
> *Beverly, government analyst*

We have a clear understanding of how money and job determine our future. What will we do about it?

> As we are turning forty, we don't have the young
> people coming up in numbers to support us in our
> old age. And that is a very strong reality, and any-
> body who is turning forty and doesn't feel that is
> going to have a big surprise. We are still going to

have a big surprise because I don't think we'll be
able to prepare for it.

I think we realize we are going to live a long
time. Medical science can keep us going into our
nineties. Even when we're old, we're younger than
we used to be.

My dad at seventy-four doesn't look like my
grandfather did at seventy-four. And this got me
thinking that we are going to have to work and we
are not going to be able to retire when we are
sixty-five. I think my father knew when he was
sixty-five he would plug into Social Security and
everything would be fine. We know now at forty
years old that it isn't going to be available to us.
Martin, author

Many of us have lived with the misguided idea that our house will be
our pension plan. We watched in astonishment as the house our parents
bought for a few thousand dollars multiplied in value over their lifetime.
We didn't notice that it multiplied because of us.

There were so many Baby Boomers competing for a limited housing
stock that house prices shot up. A psychological bandwagon effect set in
whereby we pushed prices even higher, in the expectation that they
would go higher still.

Twenty years from now, there will be fewer people buying new houses. We will have outgrown our larger homes in which we raised children
and be looking for something smaller. Yet, we continue to behave as if
the bubble will never burst.

We bought a house and that is one reason why
money is so important. The house is a symbol of
how to make a chunk of money. It symbolizes
financial independence.
Christian, plumber

A house is more than an investment. It is a roof over our heads, a
secure place we can call our own. For many forty-year-olds who haven't

bought by now, the dream may be elusive.

> I'm thinking about buying a house, but because I
> never got married and never really used to save
> when I was younger, I don't have enough money.
> The concept of living in a co-op or living with
> other people as I get older was a horror to me and
> now I am beginning to think, well, maybe that is
> the way of the future.
>
> Maybe that is what I'll have to endure and I'm
> beginning to think that, maybe, if I am old and
> lonely, it won't be an endurance. It might be fun.
> Hippies used to live together in communes. They
> smoked dope. Maybe we'll be old people taking
> some kind of cheaper, synthetic drug together.
> *Sara, airline reservations agent*

In some ways, age sixty-five feels so far away. But when the penny drops and I remember that it is a mere twenty-five years from forty, it really makes me think. Sometimes, I hear the Beatles singing "Will you still need me, will you still feed me when I'm sixty-four?" but usually I get perspective on the situation.

I start with the obvious. When I was twenty, I thought forty was so old as to be unimaginable. Now that I am over forty, I realize that age and state of mind are very closely related. If I stay in shape and take care of myself, there is no reason that sixty-five should be old. I may have a few more gray hairs and move a little slower, but I can enjoy life fully. Of course, it will require some planning up front. Clearly I have to make sure that my finances are in order to provide some fall-back position for the day I stop working, voluntarily or involuntarily. But there is a bigger investment I can make — in my health. And it doesn't cost a lot of money.

Be Here Now

Thinking about money all the time can be dangerous. It throws life out of balance, focusing on material things. We have been warned against this by most of the great religious teachers, including Jesus and Buddha. Why have they warned us against it?

Because overconcentration on material possessions blinds us to our bodies and deafens us to our hearts. If we paid more attention to our bodies, would we work twelve hours a day? Would we skip meals, refuse to exercise, and eat unhealthy things? Probably not.

At forty, we are having second thoughts about our focus on money. We are realizing that if we don't have good health, we won't be able to enjoy any material things. That's why a focus on health takes on a special importance at forty.

Health and Staying Alive

Staying Alive

Many of my forty-year-old friends are surprised they have lived this long. They are even more surprised by what has happened to their bodies.

There is more fat around the middle. Reflexes are slower. It takes longer to negotiate three flights of stairs, and the body is huffing and puffing at the top.

Mornings are punctuated by snaps and cracks as the body gets out of bed. During the day, things seem to be moving a bit too fast — mute testament to slowed reflexes. At dinner, rich, fatty foods don't sit as well in the stomach; the extra glass of wine leads to sleepiness instead of euphoria; and an early bedtime doesn't seem like such a bad idea after all. We are slowing down. For the first time in our lives, the body can't keep up with the mind.

While this subtle, inevitable metabolic change is rolling on, we are often hit by sledgehammer reminders of our mortality.

At forty, at least half of us have lost a parent. We know death comes. Even more shocking, many of us have lost acquaintances the same age. Death is often sudden, following a virulent flu or a seemingly routine hospital test that uncovers a rapidly advancing carcinoma.

We watch an uncle die of lung cancer and ask ourselves how long we can continue smoking. We see a heart attack strike an overweight relative and ask ourselves how long we can fool ourselves about the consequences of an unhealthy diet.

We care because, having reached forty, we have decided that life is worth living. Finally, we have figured out enough to take control of our lives and have some real fun. It would be terribly unfair to die now, just when it is all getting started.

And so, the struggle begins. Exercise? Cut down on fatty foods? Increase vitamin intake? Give up the cigarettes and booze? Where does it start and where does it end?

Part of the problem stems from the fact that physical change sneaks up on us slowly. Sometimes, it doesn't seem worth paying attention. We gain a couple of pounds a year, and before we know it we've grown comfortable with a little more weight, a little more stomach, and a little less energy. Some time during this insidious process, we decide we really have to do something to get in shape.

We know the road to health is paved with good intentions, so we intend to do something good for ourselves soon. But have we done anything about our health?

Watcha Gonna Do about It?

Most of us have done little to improve our physical fitness recently. More than half of those surveyed did little or nothing to improve their physical fitness within the past year. In spite of all the warnings, admonitions, and pleas by government, doctors, health club operators, and Jane Fonda and Cher, we just haven't quite stirred ourselves out of the car seat or our favorite TV-watching chair to do something about it.

Fewer than 20 percent of us say we have done "a lot" to improve our physical fitness. Among this group, there is a direct relationship between education and improving fitness. The more education we have, the more improvement.

A much greater percentage of us *intend* to do something next year to improve our physical well-being. Nearly a third of those surveyed "intend" to do a lot more "next year" to improve physical fitness. Once again, the more education we have, the more likely we are to be planning to make a big change next year.

Okay. We should be taking better care of ourselves. But have things really changed, or are we just doing the same amount of exercise we did at age thirty?

When asked "Do you now do the same amount of exercise as you did ten years ago?" nearly 40 percent of us said we do less. Only 30 percent do more exercise and, of this group, the majority are women.

Women are taking care of themselves better than men. Whether they are motivated by vanity or are simply more sensible, the fact is that women are doing more about getting in shape.

Every time I pick up a health journal, I want to scream. It's so obvious that regular physical exercise helps reduce risk of heart disease, stroke, and all sorts of nasty illnesses that can really take the fun out of life. But our modern world is built in such a way that it is really hard to get regular exercise without making a big effort.

Less than seventy years ago, before the car took over our lives, we had to walk to get from one place to another. For most of us, this meant we got regular exercise in day-to-day living. But the advent of the car and its monstrous progeny, the subdivision, meant an end to the easy integration of exercise in the daily routine. Instead of walking three blocks to a friend's house, we drive. Instead of walking to a restaurant, we take the car, because there are no sidewalks. And, of course, the more we drive, the less interest we have in sidewalks and healthy ways to keep us locomoting.

Perhaps the most ridiculous example of all is Saturday afternoon at the shopping center. We drive around for fifteen minutes, looking for a parking space that is thirty feet closer to the mall entrance. Although we try to convince ourselves that we want the closer space to save time, the reason is that we have an almost pathological aversion to walking. This healthiest exercise of all is made more difficult by our modern way of life.

We don't walk and we don't do a lot of physical labor. More of the hard, physically demanding jobs have been taken over by machines. Our information age requires brains more than muscles.

So, if we want to exercise, we have to get a home machine or join a club. In this way, exercise becomes detached from function. At least when we are walking, we are going somewhere, with a destination in mind. If we are building muscles by digging out tree stumps or carrying rocks to clear a field, we feel like we are doing something, working toward a goal.

Machine exercise is sterile, detached, a matter of checking the pulse with a fancy watch or counting the interminable moves up and down on the Stairmaster. Is it any wonder that modern-day exercise feels unsatisfying, that it might do some good for the body but doesn't do a lot for the soul? Yet, it's a matter of life and death that we make sure we exercise regularly, especially as we enter our forties.

But exercise alone can't keep us healthy. Many other variables are equally critical, including the constitution with which we were born.

Illness as Metaphor

I was a sickly child.

Two months premature, I clung to life, first in an incubator and then fighting a series of pneumonias that tried to knock me down. My health got so bad that, when I was five, my parents moved to Canada from England, hoping that cleaner air and a healthier climate would do something to revitalize my ailing lungs. Canada helped only a bit.

In public school, I missed so much time because of sickness that it is amazing I got through. In high school, things got a bit better, but I was still plagued by too many colds, strep throats, and abdominal problems. That was the bad part.

The good part was that I spent a lot of time in bed, reading, which contributed to higher grades in school and a shot at going to university. Ironically, in spite of pretty good grades, I don't remember them as the high point of my high school career. Rather, it was an improvement in my health that stands out.

Grade 12 was the first year since kindergarten in which I did not miss a day of school because of illness. I still remember the January morning that might have been the turning point.

I felt terrible. I had a bad sinus infection and a cough, and there was a test scheduled at school that day. There was no better excuse for crawling under the covers and telling my mother I was too sick to go to school. But I had to go. I had a crush on a girl in another class and I knew she would be having lunch in the cafeteria. For over a week, I had planned how I would finally get up the nerve to sit down beside her and start a conversation. No amount of sickness was going to stop me.

I put on my coat and gloves and walked a mile and a half to school in a brutal snowstorm. Frozen, coughing and sneezing, I staggered into class only to find out that my teenage fantasy would not be fulfilled. The girl I had planned to meet was home for two weeks with chicken pox!

At the end of the day, I went home, drank a few cups of warm lemonade, and went to bed. The next day I went to school. I didn't miss another day after that. I had discovered the power of the mind (and the libido!) in dealing with illness.

Over the years, I was hit by various sicknesses, including a hiatus hernia, psoriasis, a frightening asthma attack, and the usual round of colds, flus, and sinus problems. In the beginning, I accepted them as inevitable, necessary, and even nature's way of telling me to slow down. But, as I got older, I didn't like what I saw ahead.

There were too many debilitated, sickly older people. Many had brought on their own problems through neglect of diet, exercise, and healthy working conditions. Others had added fuel to the fire with cigarettes, alcohol, and drugs. I figured that if I had lived this long, I may as well try to live longer still. I decided to find out why some people got sick and others didn't.

The subject of that research would fill another book, but the condensed findings are simple.

Some people have plain bad luck. Genetically, they draw a short straw. Whatever it is — a disease, a weakness in the immune system, or something else — their life is a struggle that they may or may not win.

Some are unlucky enough to work in dangerous jobs such as asbestos or gold mining, or construction. Environmental and occupational hazards combine to put them at risk. They have a tough row to hoe.

I have also learned that a genetic short straw is not necessarily catastrophic. Allergies can be controlled through drugs and diet, and a faulty heart valve can be repaired by surgery. Even vitamins can help.

Dr. Linus Pauling, two-time Nobel Prize winner, has made a compelling case that carefully measured doses of megavitamins can help those unlucky enough not to have been born with the constitution of an ox. Dr. Donn Gaudin has shown that a better understanding of amino acids, the body's building blocks, can contribute to a healthier and better life.

On the fitness front, everyone from Jack Lalane to Jane Fonda has demonstrated that regular physical exercise goes a long way to keeping the body toned and healthy.

But, on the whole, I have learned that genes, occupation, and exercise are a small part of health, compared to the illnesses we bring on ourselves.

In the beginning, I resisted the concept that we could be responsible in any way for our own illnesses. It frightened me, made me angry, and generated a huge wall of denial. When I was sick, I was really sick. There was nothing artificial about it. How in the world could I be blamed for what was happening to me? It was a monstrous thought.

My life was turned around by a slim blue volume entitled *Heal Your Body* by Louise Hay. She didn't blame anyone for anything. Rather, she pointed out that certain types of illnesses tended to take place when a specific emotional state was present. Stomach problems might be a result of having to "digest" too many ideas or too much input all at once. Allergies might be compounded by irritation to people close by. The list went on and on. Remarkably, each time I had a physical problem, the book seemed to describe a corresponding emotional state almost identical to the one I was in at the time.

More important, the book suggested positive "affirmations" that could help unblock the negative mind set that contributed to the illness. It suggested that most illness was a result of criticism, resentment, and anger. By loving oneself, approving of oneself, and taking charge of the creative force in one's own life, one could reduce illness.

This is not to suggest that a thin book of symptom/cause relationships will replace medicine, but, rather, that we must focus on the relationship between our emotions and our health if we are to make the best of middle age.

Unfortunately, many of us don't really want to be well. We have internalized our anger, criticism, and resentment so deeply that we welcome illness.

> Sometimes, I think that sickness is a result of emotions that don't get expressed. Like when a business executive has his whole life fall apart, with his wife leaving him and his business go down.
>
> Rather than tell everyone he is in pain, cry, and show how hurt he is, he gets sick. That way, he gets all the sympathy and attention for his pain without having to tell anyone how much he's hurting. Instead, he lets the sickness do it for him.
> *Richard, therapist*

Of course, we could say that Richard's businessman's sickness is a result of stress. But what is stress?

Stress is nothing more than emotions — the body's chemical response and its consequences. Short-term and long-term stress are both destructive. By understanding ourselves better, by accepting that we are not mere victims of illness and disease, but that we can do something about it, we have a very good chance of making the second half of life even better than the first.

Lines on the Mirror, Lines on the Face

Good doctors tell us that our sense of self-worth and importance is vital to good health. In other words, if we feel good about ourselves, we are likely to be healthier.

In this image-dominated, skinny-obsessed, youth-oriented society, aging doesn't necessarily make us feel good about ourselves. In fact, gray hairs and a few wrinkles can make us feel profoundly bad.

And gray hair and wrinkles are the first thing most of us notice about aging.

Here we are, the generation that never trusted anyone over thirty, suddenly staring at gray strands in the mirror. Among women, it has been acceptable since time immemorial to dye hair. Among men, it has usually been considered suspect. Now, all that is changing. Men, too, want to look good.

I have looked at my eyes and my face and then
looked at a picture of myself at twenty-six and
thought, why don't I get rid of these wrinkles. I
mean, it can be done. I haven't put it out of my
mind. I might do it now, or maybe when I'm fifty.

What's stopping me is I keep thinking it's a sign
of inadequacy or some level of paranoia. I don't
want to go out and make myself look like a thirty-
year-old when in fact I'm not. But I think that plastic surgery is sort of like a hairpiece in the 1960s
or 1970s, when people used to laugh about it. It
can preserve your natural self and make you look
better. I haven't put it out of my mind.
Carl, physician

No matter how much men worry about their looks, women worry
much more. They carry a weighty history of women's value being equat-
ed with youthfulness and looks. As a generation, we endorsed the idea
that youth is beautiful as long as we were young. Now, as we enter our
forties, we will start to rewrite the book, focusing on the great things
about middle age.

But many women won't be able to let go of the old baggage and will
try to be teenagers long after that time is gone. More troubling, they will
continue to be sucked into the idea that the only thing that matters is
how we look.

One of the things that's really weird is the loss of
self-esteem that comes with aging. The concept of
vanity. The idea that we're a nation of middle-aged
girls.

All around, it saddens me to see women resort-
ing to surgery and much more dire artifices than
they have ever used in order to maintain their
attractiveness to the men they claim they are not
interested in. There is a real double standard in
what they're doing.

I see these emaciated little women who are

practically anorexic pumping their tiny little muscles up at the club, stretching what is left of their skin on their arms; they have sports injuries, they are too thin, and their faces look ravaged because they are over forty and they don't have any plumpness.

You know, at forty, the standard phrase says, "At forty a woman has to choose between her figure and her face." I am really seeing the results of this.

It's weird, but I'm noticing more women who want to look like men. And it bothers me that if a woman is successful, they say she has masculine traits.

Jane, antique dealer

Mother's Little Helpers

Staying healthy means keeping the body in balance. Energy in must equal energy out. It's a nice theory, but it's hard to practice in our crazy, hurry-up world. Everywhere we turn, there seem to be more demands on us than we can meet. The withdrawals at the energy bank are enormous.

Rather than cut back on trying to have everything all at once, we push ourselves harder and harder, cutting back on sleep, drinking more coffee, and promising ourselves that we will take a break soon.

During the late 1970s and through much of the 1980s, America was startled by the widespread cocaine "problem" among Baby Boomers. Of course, the moralists were all eager to suggest that cocaine was a conspiracy foisted upon an unwilling American public. It is much more likely that cocaine *seemed* to be a solution to almost inexhaustible demands on energy.

A segment of the Baby Boom, the most reckless experimenters, decided to try this new wonder drug to see if it could help them get with the thicket of demands they had to crawl through every day. For a while, it seemed possible to work all day and play all night. Cocaine seemed to be a way to have their cake and eat it too. However, it wasn't long before they discovered that those overdrafts at the energy bank came with a high interest rate. As soon as they learned it, they behaved true to form. Cocaine went out of fashion.

As Baby Boomers quit the experiment, demand went down, just as supply had gone up enormously. This meant cheap cocaine flooded the country, providing a temporary escape for angry, disenfranchised inner-city youth. Crack cocaine had arrived — an unfortunate byproduct of experimentation.

But the attraction to cocaine, even experimentally, was a symptom of the fact that we couldn't deal with the idea we no longer have the reserves of energy we had when we were young. At twenty, we wasted energy just as we waste gasoline and electricity today, thinking it will go on forever. By forty, we face the uncomfortable fact that we have to become efficient with the use of our energy rather than just burning it out.

> I used to be quite the party animal. I was a guy
> that would go out and go crazy all night long and
> then go to work the next day. And then, in my
> mid-thirties I found myself not bouncing back
> from those late nights the way I once did.
>   Suddenly I had two-day hangovers, and one
> good night's sleep was no longer enough to fix me
> up. I thought I'd better start taking care of myself
> like the old Groucho Marx line "If I knew that I
> was going to live this long, I would have taken bet-
> ter care of myself." Well, I am trying to do that
> now.
> *Juan, pipe fitter*

No matter how much our logic tells us that we shouldn't do drugs to give us back energy, there is one addiction we have real difficulty kicking — coffee.

> I find I drink way too much coffee, and it's a sort of
> psychological dependence. It gives me a brief thrill
> and is a great reason not to exercise. It gives you a

little physical buzz without actually doing anything for yourself. So I'm trying to be aware of it
and cut that out. Coffee and cigarettes are pretty
innocent fixes, but they're still very pernicious
downers in the morning.
Alex, university admissions

Coffee is a boost, an upper, a bridging loan at the energy bank. But
our other legal drugs are more damaging still, especially cigarettes. At
forty, almost everyone who smokes is trying to give up, and it isn't easy.
We range all the way from outright addicts trying to kick the habit to
closet smokers who have kept it from their kids for years.

My kids don't know it, but I'm sort of a closet
smoker and I'm trying to cut back on that. I don't
like to smoke in front of them because I don't want
them to smoke. I've been smoking for thirty years,
and I smoke four or five cigarettes a day without
anybody really knowing about it. I've got to cut
back.
Mel, accountant

I've smoked cigarettes on and off most of my adult
life. I've quit several times for extended periods,
for a couple of years at a time, but somehow I
always back-slid into it. It bothers me more now
because of my son.

I don't like to smoke in front of him, and I
remember being influenced by my father, who was
a smoker, when I was a youth, and I am sure that
had an effect on me, on the fact that I smoke now.
So, it is very much on my mind to give it up.
Frank, airline pilot

I have no doubt that cigarette smoking will continue to decline as we
get older. It is losing its status. When a drug loses status, the effect slowly filters down all the way through the population, and overall consumption goes down. To a much lesser extent, the same thing will happen

with coffee drinking. A small group of ultra-hip experimenters will begin trying out caffeine-free herb teas and other benign hot beverages. Within ten years, we will see significant changes — a decline in coffee consumption and growth in popularity of the alternatives.

To a certain extent, the same is true of our other legal drug — alcohol. At twenty, we found that alcohol was great for getting rid of inhibitions. In the right quantities, it freed us to get on with the most important things in life at that age — partying and sex. But, over time, whether we like it or not, most of us notice the effects of alcohol as one of the early signs that something is changing as we age.

> With alcohol I found that, lately, in the past few years, the recovery period is worse. That my hangovers are worse and that the next day after some hard partying I don't have quite the energy I used to have. So, that is making me leave it a bit alone.
>
> Maybe there are parts of my insides that are saying "That is enough." So, I haven't had a drink for a couple of months, and the first thing I noticed is how much more energy I had when I didn't drink.
>
> *Jean, sculptor*

Cigarettes, alcohol, and coffee could be thought of as bad drugs, mother's little helpers that are doing more harm than good. On the flip side, as we age, we get more interested in perceived good drugs, such as vitamins and natural substances found in food. For most of us, it is very likely that, as we age, we will search out the fountain of youth in the vitamins, amino acids, kelp extracts, and every other weird promise that comes in a bottle. It is part of a trend toward self-medication.

As the most educated, experimental generation in history, we sometimes know more than our doctors. After all, research findings coming out of the lab today won't find their way into medical schools for at least ten years and might not become part of general medical practice for another twenty. It is in our best self-interest to keep up with research on aging.

Doctors often tell us that we should let them do the thinking for us, that we don't have the training to determine what is right and what is wrong. These are the same doctors who told us thirty years ago that there was no evidence that cigarette smoking was really harmful; that regularity in the bowels wasn't such a big deal; and that most allergies were psychological. Is it any wonder that we feel our survival hinges on keeping ourselves really well informed?

The danger comes when a news-starved press suddenly reports startling discoveries, such as the fact that aspirin seems to reduce the incidence of fatal second heart attacks. If we don't read the fine print carefully, we might be setting ourselves up for one disease while trying to prevent another.

> I take an aspirin a day because I read something in
> the paper that it might prevent heart attacks. I take
> a vitamin a day from the health food store, a pretty
> healthy vitamin, and usually it keeps me pretty
> healthy.
> *Jillian, house painter*

So, good health becomes a balancing act. We try to eat the right foods, take the right drugs, and keep ourselves in balance. We poke around with amino acids and other touted life extenders, hoping to give ourselves more energy, a longer life, and a better sense of well-being.

> I feel that I need a Valium more times than I need
> vitamins. But I have an ageless image. So, I have
> bought things I would never have bought before in
> my life, like Ageless Image amino acid tablets.
> Things like that, you know.
> *Aileen, receptionist*

A Valium more than a vitamin. How many of us feel that way some days, when the stress just seems to be too much? More important, as a generation, how are we dealing with stress, the factor that we can't quite measure but that we all know contributes to sickness and even death?

Running on Empty

We know stress kills. We develop more stress from hearing about how stressful stress can be. Stress breeds stress. We are a stress-obsessed generation.

Or so the media tell us. Is it true?

At forty, more than half of us say we have more stress than we did ten years ago. A lucky 20 percent of us feel less stress. In other words, at forty we are more stressed out than we were at thirty.

And we can't escape stress by moving to a small town or earning more money because forty-year-olds in small towns feel just as stressed as their counterparts in big cities, and forty-year-olds who earn more than $50,000 a year feel just as stressed as those who earn less than $30,000 a year.

So, what causes stress? When asked what they considered the number-one source of personal stress, men surveyed put their jobs at the top of the list.

Causes of Stress for Forty-Year-Old Men

Job	53%
Money	22%
Home: Children	8%
Marital	6%
Health	4%

Money is far behind job as a source of stress for men. For women, job is still number one, but money and children run a very close second.

Causes of Stress for Forty-Year-Old Women

Job	34%
Money	25%
Home: Children	22%
Marital	12%
Health	7%

For both men and women, the more money we make, the more likely our job is to be the biggest source of stress. The less money we make, the more likely money is to be the biggest source of stress. But, stress is stress whether caused by money or job.

We have more stress than our parents' generation because there are more opportunities to be stressed out. Technology gives us the chance to communicate with one another twenty-four hours a day anywhere in the world. Transportation runs twenty-four hours a day. A global marketplace means that we have to think about the fact that it is 9:00 a.m. in Hong Kong when we're just sitting down to have dinner. A lot of the old physical barriers between time and space have fallen. It creates tremendous opportunities, but it means that we have to be on our toes all the time, balancing schedules, expectations, family life, and even the demands of our own bodies.

For me, as for most men, job seems to be the biggest source of stress, because it doesn't allow me enough regularity in my life. I get on airplanes and fly all over the country; sleep in strange hotels with awful pillows and unusual noises; sit through interminable breakfast, lunch, and dinner meetings; bounce from time zone to time zone — and often wonder if it's all worth it.

As well as physical stress, there is mental stress. Keeping clients happy, managing employee performance, trying to find time for my wife and even time for myself. It all adds up.

The bottom line seems to be: most stress comes from trying to make other people happy. That might sound selfish, but it's true. We worry more about what other people think of us, feel about us, and do to us than we do about what is important for us personally. Of course, it's easy to be philosophical about it — until we have to worry about keeping the boss happy for fear of losing our job. But it is exactly that kind of worry that wears us down.

In order to stay healthy, we have to reduce stress, to release a safety valve on our psyche that will restore the equilibrium. How do we do it?

Let's Get Physical

The number-one choice in stress-reduction tactics among forty-year-olds is physical activity — working stress off by working it out. It was *the* approach for nearly 25 percent of forty-year-olds surveyed. And the greater the education, the greater the likelihood of using physical activity to get rid of stress — probably because the stress results from a job based on mental work behind a desk.

Physical activities help to reduce stress while toning up muscles and the cardiovascular system.

Following close behind as the number-two way of reducing stress is some form of personal leisure activity, such as gardening, fishing, sewing, or camping. Nearly 25 percent of those surveyed reduce physical stress this way. Interestingly, the more education you have, the less likely you are to reduce stress through these kinds of personal activities.

In other words, just over half of all forty-year-olds surveyed reduce stress through physical activity. The activity might be vigorous, such as working out, or gentle, such as sewing, but it involves the body and releases the mind.

> For me, it's fishing. When I get out on that lake
> and there's nobody there but me and the morning,
> I know I'm alive. No wife, no kids, nobody yelling,
> no time clocks, just me and the fish. Then, try and
> ask me about stress.
> Bob, factory maintenance

The third choice of method for stress reduction is anything but physical — watching TV. Nearly 19 percent of forty-year-olds surveyed watch TV to reduce stress.

There is something satisfying about plopping down in front of the television set, turning off the mind, and being entertained. As we channel-hop, we feel a sense of control in our lives. A lot of our daily stress results from the feeling that we have no control, that other people push us around, whether at work or on the freeway. Punching away merrily at the buttons, flipping through forty channels, complaining that there's nothing on, we take control over our lives.

As well as offering the semblance of control, television has an almost narcotic effect on the mind. It floods us with pictures so that our imaginations can shut down, letting a series of rapidly changing images take over. There is no processing with television, no effort necessary to figure out what's going on. Unlike music or literature, TV leaves us no room to put in a part of ourself. That can be very relaxing, even though the effect is like that of a drug.

The number-three form of stress release is also a drug, but a real rather than symbolic one. Even though we know we shouldn't, just over 6 percent of forty-year-olds use alcohol, tobacco, or controlled substances to reduce stress. Translated into hard numbers, that means that at any given time, close to 250,000 forty-year-olds are using alcohol, drugs, or tobacco as the number-one way of reducing stress.

Almost as a counterpoint, numbers four and five on the list are reading and meditation and prayer. Women are four times more likely than men to read to reduce stress.

Far down the list come vacations. In spite of all the talk about taking time to have vacations, to relax and smell the flowers, barely 3 percent of forty-year-olds use them as a way of reducing stress. Amazingly, 2 percent of us work harder to get rid of stress!

We know that stress makes us feel bad. We have been told it can lead to serious illness. And we are trying to do something about it.

However, we don't usually respond to stress until we feel it physically, for example, as sore muscles, headaches, or a pain in the back. It's the body's way of telling us to pay attention. And one of the first steps to a healthier life is to take a close look at our body at forty.

I Ache in Places Where I Used to Play

The weirdest part about the body at forty is the funny sounds it starts to make in the morning. It's almost like Rice Crispies — snap, crackle, and pop.

> The one thing I've really noticed as I've gotten older is that my bones are creaking more than they used to. Any little spasm or twinge that I used to write off I now think is rheumatoid arthritis, cancer of the bone, or something like that. So I am extremely conscious about my health. I've noticed I'm aging, and I even stay out of the sun.
> *Helga, gardener*

My weight has shifted down. Without losing weight, I get love handles and a belly and a gut, and my muscle tone seems to have relaxed.

This has really impacted me because I can't exercise like I used to so I develop a lot of aches and pains and I find that I can't rent a sports car and easily get into it and out of it as I used to. It's sort of like an impotence on a whole other level.

Laim, deliveryman

I'm very annoyed at my body at the moment because it's been more than a month and I haven't completely healed from a softball injury. I'm start-ing to be more conscious of the usual aches and pains and lack of stamina for staying up nights and that sort of thing.

The weird part is that I'm starting to test myself, push the limits, see how far I can go, trying to see if I'm still young. Sometimes the results are happy, but more often they are despairing because I just can't take it anymore.

Ali, journalist

Personally, I find the snaps, crackles, and pops annoying. Sometimes, my neck sounds like pins going down in a bowling alley. My wrists pop so loud that I'm afraid I've dislocated something and, like other forties, I vow that I really intend to do something about it. I really do. I just can't seem to find the time.

Work It Out

As a self-confessed exercise avoider, I have wrestled with myself on this subject. Usually, conscience wins two out of three, and I plan that soon I really will take care of myself. Five years ago, I joined an exercise club for a year, but after drearily riding the exercycle, stepping up and down onto a box, counting my pulse, and often feeling sicker at the end of the hour than I did before I started, I decided there had to be something else.

My biggest problem with exercise clubs is the fact that they are a form of competition against yourself. Now, I am already a very competitive guy. At work and in business I compete hard. My friends and my doctor tell me that I shouldn't compete this hard, that it causes stress, so I try to cut back on competition. Then, I go to the exercise club and have to compete against myself! Is my pulse high enough? Couldn't I just put on a little more push? And this is supposed to be reducing my stress!?

I love bicycling but live in a city where it entails choking on about 10 cubic feet of diesel exhaust every block. I like swimming, but the water's so cold that I break out in goose bumps and can't move enough to get my heart rate started, let alone up to the recommended cardiovascular levels. Walking is fun, but it takes such a long time. But. But. But.

Now, my wife is shaming me by regularly attending a health club where she is turning into the woman I knew fifteen years ago. My only consolation comes from the fact that I am not alone in my struggle.

> I don't really like to exercise a lot. I've been trying to do a few sit-ups every night but I find it's hard. I feel like I'm really pushing when I do that. And the only thing that keeps me going is when a dress doesn't fit me from last year and it's one of my favorites. It just makes me mad.
> *Alena, claims adjuster*

> You know, with an office kind of job, going on sales calls and all that, you really don't get the kind of cardiovascular exercise you need. I've got a bicycle over there, right in the corner, and I intend to use it sometime soon. Occasionally, I go for walks and stuff. But my current girlfriend doesn't play tennis or anything like that, so it kind of drifts. I have to change.
> *Glen, radio salesman*

We are so resistant to exercise on an ongoing basis that it may be the death of all of us yet.

If my body doesn't start coming around soon and I
get to the point where I'm really annoyed with
myself, I may try some kind of exercise program.
But it's definitely a last resort.
Howard, VCR repairman

Okay. Whether we exercise or not, the doctors keep telling us that we have to get our cholesterol down. We have to modify our diet if we want to live long enough to worry about our old age pensions and sex life at seventy.

Eat It

If we are what we eat, there are fewer cows among us and a lot more chickens and fish. Thumbing our nose at tradition, a lot of us have declared war on red meat.

Fueled by the cholesterol scares of the 1970s, the war against beef has never abated. That is not to say that we don't eat our share of hamburgers, fajitas, and barbecued ribs. Rather, the war against beef is the tip of an iceberg with far-reaching consequences for our dietary future.

Red meat has had bad press. Associated with high-fat diets, it has never fully recovered among forties as the food of choice.

More than half of us eat less red meat than we did ten years ago, but a few hardy souls (about 5 percent) eat more.

There is a relationship between income and education and eating red meat. As your income goes up, you are less likely to eat as much red meat as you did ten years ago. As your education goes up, you are even less likely to eat red meat.

But, in spite of all the dietary scares, most of us won't change our basic way of eating. We may reorient toward less fat, more fiber, and healthier food, but as long as we feel healthy, we are going to pile on the ice cream or cut into a thick juicy steak and say to hell with the consequences.

I have a wide group of friends from the age of
twenty-four through seventy-five but the younger
people, I call them kids, if I ask them "What is

your cholesterol rate?" they could care less and
don't know what you are talking about. The people
who are in the forties group could rattle it off
immediately.

I have a low cholesterol rate, so I eat steak and
red meat four to five nights a week but also eat
corn, a lot of vegetables, fruits, ice cream, and I am
still in reasonably good health.
Owen, lumber salesman

Sometimes, the health authorities must feel like wrapping up the store and going home. In spite of more than fifteen years of publicity about the dangers of dietary fat, the message hasn't sunk in. Instead, we seem to have picked up the idea that if we cut down on red meat, we can reward ourselves with premium ice cream.

I'm trying to do something good for my diet, but
I'm still heavy on the ice cream, heavy on the
cakes. But I don't seem to put on weight, so I don't
know if it's hurting me or not. I try to keep away
from the high-cholesterol stuff — french fries and
that type of thing. Still, I drink a lot of milk and
milkshakes.
Lloyd, lab technician

It is not easy to change our dietary habits. We pick them up when we are very young, associating food with love, family connection, and comfort. If we got ice cream when we felt sick, we give ourselves ice cream to soothe emotional hurts as we get older. If Mom loved us for taking two servings of roast beef, we double up on the servings at forty, even though we aren't hungry. Most pernicious of all, if Dad threatened us unless we ate every single thing on our plate, we still clean the plate at a restaurant, even though there is enough food there for three healthy people.

It is hard to break away from habit, tradition, and conditioning. Just ask Pavlov's dogs. However, using our intelligence and making the changes slowly, many of us are moving toward a healthier diet.

I am not eating any butter at all. I am staying away
from anything that has got cholesterol in it. I drink
skim milk, I'm not eating desserts like I used to,
I'm taking better care of myself, eating less red
meat, more fish, more chicken, more salads, that
kind of stuff.
Bernie, record promoter

I am married to a guy who hasn't eaten red meat
for twenty years. And he reads every label in the
supermarket.
　　I mean, I am not as conscientious as he is about
it, but being with him has really given me a different perception of things, about reading labels and
thinking about it. We don't keep sodas in the
house anymore, or junk food for the kids.
Carmine, audiologist

Many of us won't do anything about our diet until we are shocked
into it, often by a trip to the family doctor.

My cholesterol level is high and I can't seem to get
it down. I went to a doctor and he said that he was
shocked, that my cholesterol level was way beyond
what it was supposed to be and he sat me down
and said, "Well, on Sunday mornings don't you get
up and have three eggs, four or five slices of bacon,
biscuits, gravy, a couple of glasses of milk, and for
lunch don't you love that grilled cheese and avoca-
do sandwich?" And this guy was naming all the
stuff I'd been eating for twenty years.
　　Then it dawned on me that I had never put it
into perspective that as you get older you've got to
watch what you eat. And for me, it's a real struggle
and takes a tremendous amount of will power.
Cameron, disc jockey

I have taken it one step farther: I eat vegetarian approximately four days a week. The secret has been a group of fabulous cookbooks and the willingness to experiment with and learn about new foods, particularly beans.

I never used to eat beans because they made me fart. There was nothing like a couple of blasts to clear a room and stop all conversation. Then, I found that if you change the water in which dried beans are soaking two or three times before you cook them, the substances that create gas are thrown out with the water.

A miracle — fiber and no farts. My life began to change.

From that point on, I entered a world of wonderful taste treats, amazing foods and recipes that filled me up and kept me healthy and my weight stable. Occasionally, I still hit the cheeseburgers and french fries, but now I approach them a different way. Rather than dashing to McDonald's or Burger King, I look for a super-high-quality burger with a great bun and hand-cut french fries. If I am going to break the dietary rules I want to do it in style. It's another form of status substitution.

As we turn forty, more and more of us will focus on what we put into our bodies. The more education we have, the more likely we will be to make changes. We will filter water, investigate organic foods, and jump on every food trend that comes along, whether it's oat bran or omega fatty acids. As science helps us to understand the relationship between the body, its cells, and nutrition, we are likely to be the best fed, healthiest generation in history.

Slow Down, You're Moving Way Too Fast

Everyone tells us we are moving too fast, that we are a highly stressed-out generation. They are right.

As Baby Boomers, we have been so focused on having it all that we have sometimes lost sight of the most important basics of all — love, closeness, companionship, a period of quiet solitude where we can contemplate the world around us.

Instead, we rush from home to job, from job to home, and then plop down in front of the TV.

For most of my life, I have been moving too fast, stressing myself out with too much time pressure, too much responsibility, and too much scheduling. About five years ago, I found something that worked for me. I began to experiment with yoga.

When I first heard the word *yoga*, I had visions of towel-headed weirdos lying on a bed of nails or chanting from sun-up to sundown. The reality was refreshingly different.

Yoga is a form of dynamic exercise that integrates body, breathing, and mind. The postures, which appear to be static, are having a remarkable effect on the organs, such as liver, gall bladder, and kidneys, as well as on important muscles, such as the heart.

Over the past five years, I have discovered that yoga can lower blood pressure and improve health and well-being, all without drugs. In the beginning, it takes a little getting used to, but over the long haul it has paid personal dividends for me. Based on my own experience, it seems like an important solution for people who are always in a hurry and never take any time to slow down. By doing a simple yoga breathing exercise for ten minutes, the body can be brought back to a healthy state of equilibrium. And the exercises can be done anywhere, without equipment or formal facilities.

Most important for me, yoga has brought my mind and spirit closer together. For the first time in my life, I feel like my body and mind are friends rather than competitors. I don't try to override myself the way I once did to "get the job done." Surprisingly, the more I slow down, the more successful I am.

I recognize that yoga is not going to appeal to most of us. There are other ways to stay healthy.

If we are going to be the healthiest generation in history, then we need to integrate our minds and bodies more effectively than we have. One of the simplest ways of all is to slow down, to develop interests outside of work, to have a hobby.

> I have always considered it important to have a life
> outside the office. I play golf, for example. Not
> very well, but I play. And I try to keep that sepa-
> rate and apart from my business as much as possi-
> ble. If I do play golf with a business acquaintance,
> it is purely on a social level.

> Things I do with my son, activities that he is
> involved with, such as soccer, little league, and
> those kind of things, have absolutely nothing to do
> with my business. And I find it healthy. It is almost
> like a mental enema.
> *Eraldo, advertising executive*

If it is so easy to develop hobbies and slow down, why don't we? Why is it so hard for us to take a few moments away from the job or the family and say "This is just for me"? The answer lies in our Protestant work ethic.

Somewhere along the way, almost all of us have heard a parent, aunt, or uncle say, "The devil makes work for idle hands" or "Hard work never killed anyone." Of course, neither quote is true. But we aren't a very introspective nation, so we never question such destructive statements. Instead, we internalize them and then turn around and pride ourselves on the fact that we don't take much vacation or that we stay at the office until 8:00 at night. What madness!

I knew a manager who proudly told me that he had never taken a vacation in twenty-two years. Four months later, his company rewarded him for this loyalty by firing him. Yes, he had turned up for work faithfully for twenty-two years. But he had never been able to relax or get far enough away from his job to give himself perspective on it. As a result, he kept doing everything the same way he always had, unexposed to new ideas, unrefreshed by a good spell of time to let the mind go blank.

It is dangerous to our mental and physical health to measure our self-worth by the number of hours we put in at a job. Instead, we should look at the number of productive hours, the time when we actually get something done.

We are much more likely to do a real, full day's work if we are rested than if we simply turn up at the factory or the office and go through the motions because we haven't had any time off.

One of the most important things we can do at forty is take a real, hard look at holidays and time off. The Germans have long vacations every year and are one of the most efficient producing countries in the world. If we are to live a long time, we should take more of it to stop and smell the flowers.

I have a high-stress job so I am real careful to be
very liberal with my vacations. I take a lot of vacations. If I need a day off, I take it. Or, I might stay
at home in the morning to keep myself grounded
and balanced and then go in and do battle in the
afternoon. I do a lot of things consciously to take
care of myself in that way.
Cindy, shipping manager

The good news about forty is the fact that we learn to accept ourselves. We become more comfortable with who we really are. That takes
a lot of stress away and helps us to stay healthy.

More of us recognize the relationship between a healthy mind, self-
confidence, and a healthy body. It lets us feel more vital, gives us more
zing, and provides a sunnier outlook on life.

We look around and see other forty-year-olds with love handles, lines
on the face, and a few gray hairs. We might have gained a few pounds,
but so has everybody else. We shed the narrow criticism of youth based
on looks and image and move a little deeper into ourselves. It's a good
thing.

I'm generally very healthy except that I have
gained weight in the last year and I am not as
physically active as I should be and that's not good
because exercise would help me deal with stress.

I feel better about myself. I am still vain and I
think I am a little inhibited although I'm not as
inhibited as I was twenty years ago. I realize now
what sex appeal is all about.

I mean, a woman can be beautiful and stunning
and have not much to her personality and be treated as an adornment and nothing more by men. But
the women who have satisfying and interesting sex
lives are those who have a zest and a zeal for life,
and it doesn't matter which form or figure they
come in.
Trish, librarian

Chances Are

Even if we don't exercise as much or take really good care of ourselves, we are likely to be the longest-lived generation so far in history.

If you are a woman of forty, you have one chance in five of living to be ninety. That means fifty more years to do something with your life. Here are the odds:

Chances of living to age...	Male	Female
	%	%
80	37	57
90	9	23
100	0.4	1.5

If we average it out, a forty-year-old male is likely to live to be almost seventy-five, while a forty-year-old female is likely to live to be just over eighty.

With a long life in front of us, it is obvious we need to consider money and jobs as well as health. But, for most of us, the biggest surprise will be the fact that we have an active sex life as we get older.

Sex

You Can't Always Get What You Want, But If You Try Sometime, You Just Might Find, You Get What You Need

Good news.

There is sex after forty.

In fact, most of us enjoy sex more now than we did ten years ago. The bad news is that the enjoyment comes at a price.

Most of us have sex less often than we did at thirty. We've traded quality for quantity.

The most sexually active forties are those who are single and in a relationship. If you are one of the lucky ones, you are doing it more and enjoying it more. Who said sex at forty can't be fun?

The big difference between sex at thirty and sex at forty is centered on the fact that our experience has widened and our expectations have subtly shifted. We have a much better idea of what it takes to make us sexually happy. We have discovered this by chance or design.

Chance is just plain luck. A divorce may have started us dating again with clearer ideas of what we wanted sexually in a relationship. With luck, we found the right person.

Design is another word for learning. For many of us, our sex life has improved because we have learned about it. There are books, courses, radio and TV shows that discuss sex. The taboo topic for our parents has become commonplace for our generation.

We are getting to the age where memory gets a good workout. With sufficient perspective, we can look back on our sexual adventures and misadventures, trying to fit them into our day-to-day life. We have started to make compromises within both marriage and relationships.

Was it really less than twenty years ago when "swinging" was considered a great idea, when "open" marriages meant that husbands and wives could sleep with whomever they wanted, when sex clubs were a weekend's fun for bored suburban couples? Most of that experimentation has disappeared or gone underground, driven by fear of AIDS, a bit of midlife malaise, and a refocusing of priorities toward job and family.

At the grass-roots level, the sex haters have been doing a wonderful job of stirring up politicians and the media against sex. They have almost succeeded in making it a crime to hug a child too closely, to enjoy erotica in the privacy of your own home, and to feel good about the human body. I wouldn't be surprised if this group tries to make sex between seventy-year-olds an "affront to the dignity of aging" by the time we get there.

But we are unlikely to fight back as much as we used to. We watch in horror as our children are exposed to sex and violence on network television. We find it difficult to explain daytime soap operas to them. And so, rather than deal with these difficult issues, to personally try to make sense of them to our children, we gradually let the right to our own sexuality slip away under the guise of morality. It would be a lot better if we talked openly with our children about sex rather than letting them discover it through a combination of Mickey Rourke movies and the backseat of a car.

The fact that we are still uncomfortable talking about sex with our children suggests that we haven't fully come to grips with our sexuality. For a large minority, it is easier to ignore it than deal with it.

Although most of us enjoy sex more than we did ten years ago, a growing number are giving up on sex completely. Celibacy is the result. Now that our chins, breasts, and bellies sag a bit, it's easier to let go, pretending that sex doesn't matter at all. Among forties surveyed, 7 percent hadn't had sex for more than a year. Even more surprising, among married forty-year-olds, 3 percent hadn't had sex for more than a year. And among singles not in a relationship, 26 percent hadn't had sex for more than a year.

To put this in perspective, 65 percent of us have had sex within the last week. So, things aren't that bad.

As all this change takes place, we try to remember whether sex was really as good twenty years ago. We try to remember the intensity and forget the pain.

By age forty, sex is tangled up in a net of memories, suppressed desire, physical change, marriage pressures, increased awareness, and mortal reminders of the danger of disease.

Our net has been snagging on sex for at least twenty years. It has snagged on love, passion, loss, pain, pleasure, joy, and fear. At last, at age forty, we have perspective, a chance to try to make sense of it all.

If we pulled the net out of the water now, what might we find?

The Spirit Is Willing, But the Flesh Is Weak

Like it or not (and most of us don't like it), the body changes as we age.

Among women, the lining of the vaginal walls thins, hormone production changes, lubrication decreases, and menstruation becomes more irregular.

Among men, there is a drop in levels of testosterone, changes in the circulation of the blood, and a drop in the sperm count.

None of these changes detracts from sexual pleasure, though sometimes they force us to pause a moment longer before we get on with the fun.

At age forty, experience has to do some of the work the body used to do. The journey takes a little more time, but the destination is more rewarding.

Most of us are more comfortable in our sexuality. We are no longer held hostage by out-of-control hormones and peer-group pressure.

Over time, we have figured out the two important secrets of sex: we know what makes us feel good and we aren't afraid to ask for it.

> For me, turning forty, sex has gotten better. We've
> gotten out of the back seat of a car in high school

and the anxious moments. It's more relaxed. There
is no hurry.

I think that for myself I can enjoy it more at
this particular stage of the game than I did back at
twenty, or even thirty. It's just gotten better as the
years have gone by.
Vincent, furniture sales

I feel much more comfortable than ever before in
my whole life with my own sexuality. The only
interesting thing is there is no one in my life. Here
I am, I have all this to offer, and there's no one to
take advantage of it.
Suzette, cosmetician

Of course, there are those of us who have still never made the big
connection.

They say when you get older, it's supposed to get
better, right? Maybe it is. It's okay. Really, it's about
the same.
Gabriella, housewife

Some of us are so all-out excited about the growth of sexual experience that we want to share it with the world.

One thing about being forty is that you have had a
few partners or at least a bit of experience. You're
an accomplished love-maker. And I do consider
myself that. I have had a lot of women who have
been very happy with me and I often wish for that
reason alone that I could screw a lot more women
because I know I could do an excellent job of it.

It's a ridiculous way to feel perhaps because it's
very arrogant or at least very foolish or self-deni-
grating in a sense too. But I feel it's my duty to
make these women happy because they are beauti-

ful and because I know I could please them. It's
not really my duty at all.
It's part of the glamour of my sexual longing.
Ray, office supplies

Ray may sound a bit pathetic, an office supply Casanova who is act-
ing like a horny teenager, but, if we look at what he says more closely, he
is making an important observation about sex: experience makes it better, and sharing can be fun. Yet, just when we get experience, we have
very few opportunities to share it.

For most of my life, I have wrestled with the question of sexual fidelity. Why should a man and woman be faithful to each other? The rapid-
response answers are that we fear disease and that religion tells us we
should be monogamous. Then, there are all the pseudo-psychological
reasons, which seem to change almost every ten years.

After thinking about it at length, I have decided that fidelity brings
sex back into perspective in marriage or a relationship. Without it, we
would be in a state of constant search for newness and excitement. We
would never get past the rush of sexual novelty to build the important,
slightly more boring, pillars of a good relationship, which include compromise, mutual respect, and shared goals. And most forty-year-olds
seem to agree.

On the whole, we are more monogamous and faithful to one person
than we were ten years ago. For most of us, it isn't a big change. More
than half of us say it's "about the same" as it was a decade ago.

However, another 25 percent of us are more monogamous than we
were ten years ago. This shift is a result of more happiness, the general
sexual slowdown that comes with age, a lessening of opportunities, and
the fear of diseases.

Most likely, as our hormones cool down a notch, we begin to look at
the larger perspective.

You always hear the cliché that if you are a man
you peak at eighteen or nineteen. It's probably
true, but the road down hasn't been like this
downward slope. I have a good sex life and it's
probably going to sound pretty boring because

before I got married, for many years I had a fairly
promiscuous life and I enjoyed it.

I'm probably really not a very oversexed person.
It amazes me how much time, energy, and effort
people spend talking about sex. I mean, for God's
sake, you do it once, twice, three times a day. It
takes up to an hour or two at the most. There are
twenty-two hours more to go!

Adam, actuary

On the whole, women are more comfortable at forty than they were
at thirty when it comes to making themselves happy sexually.

It's a lot better than when I was twenty years old.
To be really honest, in my first marriage I picked
someone who restrained my sexuality because I
was afraid of it. I was very young. I was nineteen.
And then when I was twenty-eight, I got divorced
and went through a lot of different sexual relationships, exploring. Now I am just more comfortable.

Chana, receptionist

It's changed in that it's so easy now. It's easier than
ever to orgasm.

When I was twenty, what was important to me
was security and having a boyfriend and having
Friday-night dates. You know, having somebody
take care of me and put his arm around me. Sex
wasn't even a thing. It was something that was the
thing to do. But a twenty-year-old guy, all he wants
to do is screw. For me, it completely reversed at
thirty.

At thirty, I became orgasmic. I couldn't get
enough! I didn't want anyone taking care of me. I
could take care of myself just fine. And as I became
more confident about myself and more relaxed
sexually, it all started to happen and I think it is

partly physical but 70 percent emotional.
Lucille, fashion photographer

But not all of us enjoy sex more as we age. For a minority, the urge changes. The game is too tiring. It all adds up to a big zero.

> I didn't get laid until I was nineteen. And then I
> went on this rush from the time I was about twen-
> ty-two till I got married the first time when I was
> thirty. It was countless encounters. A decade of
> one-night stands. And then I got married, and sex
> got tangled up in a lot of emotional things that I
> hadn't realized about my upbringing, about not
> having a mother and my poor sense of family. That
> really interfered with my marriage as it turns out. I
> was not used to having sex with the same women
> for seven years.
> In working this out, I realize I am not nearly as
> sexual as I used to be. I enjoy it less often now.
> And even look forward to a day when I don't have
> to have sex anymore.
> One of the nice things about getting to be forty
> is that you are not far away from giving it all up, if
> that is the way you think. Which is okay by me. I
> am very uncomfortable being forced into a sexual
> situation. Now I understand how a lot of girls
> must have felt along the way.
> *Tony, policeman*

From the moment we first noticed it, our sexuality has continued to surprise us. Through our teens and twenties, hormones were in control. By our thirties, we were starting to get perspective on what we really want out of sex.

By forty, we have traveled far enough from the explosive onset of puberty that we can look back for a moment and try to make sense of it all.

The Times They Are A-Changing

I remember my first quantum leap in sexual awareness.

I was nine years old when a group of friends dragged me into the woods to show me some naked women. In their trembling hands, they held three hurriedly torn pages from *National Geographic* magazine for me to gaze upon the forbidden object — naked breasts on tribeswomen in some remote hill district of Africa. So much for the dawning of sexuality in the 1950s.

The second quantum leap came a few years later when another friend furtively handed me a copy of *Playboy* magazine. Now this was more like it!

These naked beauties were supposed to be the girl next door. They bore no resemblance to my neighbors, who squinted over their noses, wore pageboy bobs, and giggled uncontrollably. As I held the forbidden magazine in my hand, it was impossible to imagine how fast sexual standards would change. We went from "Nice girls don't do that" to "Wanna bang?" in less than a decade.

When I began watching television, married couples were shown sleeping in separate beds. By the time cable arrived, I could sit in New York City and watch sexual behavior that would make my father blush.

We forties were swept along in a headlong wave of sexual liberation that seemed like a great idea at the time. The wave resulted from a historically unprecedented convergence of population and technological change.

First, there were a greater number of teenagers than at any period in our history. For nearly twenty years, almost 4 million teenagers a year reached puberty at the same time. That's a lot of hormones running loose at once.

Second, the transistor made radio portable.

Connecting the transistor radio to sex may seem like quite a jump, especially since the so-called experts tried to fool us into believing that television was the big force in the sexual revolution. They couldn't be more wrong.

Television was middle-class whites who slept in twin beds. The women were hairbrained. The men, with few exceptions, were steady centers of the home. Teenage children had no sexuality. In fact, sex was so threatening that Ed Sullivan wouldn't let the cameras focus on Elvis Presley below the waist when he debuted on his television show. He refused to let the Rolling Stones sing "Let's Spend the Night Together," demanding they substitute "some time" for "the night." But radio was a different story.

Until the transistor, radio wasn't portable. That meant the family radio sat in the living room, where Mom or Dad (usually Dad) decided what everyone would hear. As a result, there was no music for teenagers.

Then, the transistor hit the scene, and a portable radio became truly affordable. Advertisers were looking for a way to efficiently reach millions of new teen consumers. Top Forty radio fit the bill. For the first time, it was possible to get a radio away from parents and listen to music just for us. A lot of the music was stupid, banal, and downright awful. But a lot was wonderful, exhilarating, and liberating.

The beat was sexual. The lyrics were romantic with overtones of forbidden desire. The British invasion came, and millions of pubescent teen girls squirmed and screamed as the Beatles led the parade into the 1960s.

We had it all — music, the birth control pill, an unprecedented number of teenagers all horny at the same time, an unprecedented number of automobiles to have sex in, and, most important, a willingness to reject the old ways while searching for the new rules to guide our lives.

We became the best-educated generation in history. Education increased our awareness. Knowledge made us less afraid of sex. The taboos fell. Everyone was looking for Mr. Goodbar. Sexual liberation hit the streets.

Will You Still Love Me Tomorrow?

At forty, we are still reaping the ambiguous harvest of the sexual revolution.

On the one hand, we are less confused about sex than our parents were. Women are more comfortable expressing their needs. Men feel slightly less pressure to be macho studs.

On the other hand, we have broken marriages, new diseases, and a sense that, on the road to sexual liberation, we took a left turn and lost a little romance. Yet, when we stand back, clear headed, and look at change objectively, the sexual revolution has been good for us.

It has moved sex from duty toward pleasure. It has broken destructive taboos such as the idea that a woman shouldn't go out with a younger man. It has given us more confidence in ourselves.

> For the first time in my life I am going out with a man seven years younger than me and for the first time in my life I am asking for what I want. And I have to say that younger men are way better in this area than guys my age or older because guys my age who are just about to turn forty seem to be locked into certain ways of doing things that they have done with their wives or previous girlfriends.
>
> It started in my late thirties when, after being monogamous in every relationship, I decided I would try cheating on whoever I was going out with. It was curiously simultaneously thrilling and not satisfying at all, and what I was trying to do was feel like what it might be like from a man's point of view. Could women do that kind of thing? Could I do that type of thing without feeling guilty and tortured? And I didn't feel guilty at all.
>
> I found it incredibly fun and for the first time in my life I realized there were people out there who actually knew how to have sex with someone and make it enjoyable and interesting.
> *Laurie, film distribution*

While some of us are getting more comfortable with multiple sex partners, a larger group is coming to grips with monogamy.

> When I first got married, I thought "Boy, am I really going to spend the rest of my life with this person? And, in theory anyway, this is the only person I'll ever have sex with for the rest of my life," and that bothered me. But now it doesn't.

> It is quite a contrast to the way it was around
> that time — 1967, '68 and '69 — those so-called
> free love years when everyone was far more open.
> People were sleeping with other people more fre-
> quently and for different kinds of reasons than
> now.
> *Nick, sports lawyer*

The sexual revolution is like any other revolution. It starts with idealism, mass support, and a "throw out the rules" mentality. After a while,
the ideals of the revolution are questioned, debated, and refined.

The fires of revolution dim, and what were once monumental
changes are now taken for granted. The next generation who follow a
revolution seldom realize what was won by those who went before.

> I was at the beach last weekend and I was looking
> at those nineteen-, twenty-year-olds with slim
> hips, amazing breasts, and the skin on their faces
> looked fabulous. I thought, God damn, this is fan-
> tastic, and being so close to naked, young women
> suddenly was a whole other revelation for me
> about how much older I am.
> *Neil, oil exploration*

We are getting older. Women can go out with younger men. We realize that sex is easier to come by than it was, but we feel it is no longer
the answer. Many of us feel that we have lost something — passion, love,
romance, innocence, the specialness of the first time.

Looking for Love in All the Wrong Places

When it comes to sex, there is nothing like innocence and naivety to
pick up the thrill. That's why so many of us remember the first time,
whether we enjoyed it or not.

As teenagers, sex is inextricably linked with romance. How many
young men had to convince young women they were in love before they

would "do it"? How many young women had to convince themselves that they were in love before they would allow themselves to "do it"?

There is something magic about sexual infatuation. It's a roller-coaster of hormones, confusion, insecurity, and need that can be more powerful than many drugs. Like drugs, it can be addictive. Like drugs, it creates a high that is remembered for a long time.

Sexual infatuation and romance go hand in hand. Together, they are the Siamese twins of remembered happiness and expected joy. By the time we reach forty, our bouts of sexual infatuation have fallen off considerably. Unless we're psychosocially unbalanced, we don't go falling in and out of love every two weeks the way we did in high school.

Age forty also increases our nostalgia quotient. We begin to think back about how much better things were when we were younger, especially with sexual energy and romance. Many of us have been in marriages or relationships for a long time by age forty. The thrill of novelty, newness, and infatuation has worn off. We begin to wonder whether we are missing something, what the spark would feel like again.

> What I have discovered over the last two or three years and really culminating this year is the desire, not so much for sexual activity on the outside of marriage, but for a rekindling of romance.
>
> What I really miss is the teenage aspects of it. The holding hands, the wondering, "Does she like me?", "Where are we going to go on the next date?" That kind of thing. I think that being able to convince somebody to not necessarily fall in "love" but at least fall into heavy romantic "like" would be great.
> *Gaetan, restaurateur*

For some, the need is so powerful that we seek to re-create it over and over. We walk around in a state of romantic rut, wondering why the thrill is gone.

> Sex is still a big problem for me in a sense. It's the most glamorous thing in my life still. My fantasies and my desire for sex are great.

> But it's also very confusing because I realize it is
> a fantasy life and I don't have the morals or the
> money to be a playboy and pursue all the women,
> so I am starting to fear that I am burning a lot of
> energy there. Meanwhile, at home, I am bored.
> *Colin, bellman*

Perhaps we just get too good at making ourselves happy as we get older.

> It becomes so easy that you become lazy. That is a
> problem. It is easy to get into bed and have sex
> and be totally satisfied in five minutes. So, instead
> of building the passion and developing the seduc-
> tion, especially when you were living with some-
> body for a length of time, it just becomes another
> means of relaxing, like smoking a joint. The prob-
> lem is that you lose a lot of the passion.
>
> So, sex is as I want it on one level, and yet I am
> yearning for those major passions which don't
> happen all that often anymore.
> *Katherine, word processor*

Someone Has to Pay the Price

The price for the sexual revolution of the 1960s and '70s was the diseases of the 1970s and '80s, particularly herpes and AIDS.

We've had a wild, exhilarating roller-coaster ride on sexual freedom.
AIDS is forcing us to take another look at the cost of a ticket.

Most of us began our active sexual experimentation when the birth
control pill became readily available. For the first time in history, a generation was freed from the fear of unwanted pregnancy. Dr. Spock's generation was loose in the sexual candy store.

If the 1950s was the era of "nice girls don't do that," the 1960s and
'70s became the era of "nice girls can do that." Mothers (and a few
fathers) had drummed the fear of unwanted pregnancy into their daughters (and a few sons) as the primary reason for avoiding premarital sex.

With the threat lifted, we went on a sexual shopping spree.

For nearly twenty years, sexual freedom became the byword. More than 60 million of us reached puberty during a fifteen-year period, providing unprecedented opportunity for experimentation and change. During the 1970s, inflation wasn't the only thing that galloped out of control. Dating gave way to singles bars. The gay community redefined the bath house. Bob, Carol, Ted, and Alice were charter members of Plato's Retreat.

Inevitably, sexual experimentation led to disease. Most of it was easily controlled with modern antibiotics.

Then, nature fired the first warning shot to suggest the rules had changed. Herpes was proclaimed a national epidemic. For the first time since the mid-1960s, there was a sexually transmitted disease that defied easy cure. The singles scene began to slow down. *Time* magazine ran banner headlines about the new plague. Most of us didn't know that this was merely a precursor of the plague to come.

AIDS changed all the rules. Originally, it was ignored by narrow-minded, puritanical politicians who, with a twisted logic, imagined it was a gay disease and would stay restricted to that community. By the time they woke up, thousands were dead, and more than a million were at risk of dying.

Not surprisingly, we feel very strongly that the majority of people our age are much more cautious about sexual behavior these days. Regardless of race, income, or education, we all think the other person is taking fewer chances.

However, a weird kind of 1950s mentality still exists among too many of us. We still have the dangerously mistaken impression that we can somehow tell the "nice" people from the ones who aren't so nice, that we can detect AIDS risk based on good grooming, intelligent conversation, or family background.

Twenty years ago, this mistaken assumption might have led to gonorrhea or syphilis, followed by an inconvenient treatment with antibiotics and full recovery. These days, the inconvenience could be death.

Chance of Catching AIDS at Forty
Men   — 50 chances in 100,000
Women — 3 chances in 100,000

It is shocking to think that unprotected sex now carries the risk of death. It's particularly unsettling when we consider that half of all marriages end in divorce. This means that many of us are suddenly dating again for the first time in fifteen years as we reach our fortieth birthday.

Perhaps the most frightening thing I have seen in this survey of forties is the fact that, while we acknowledge the danger of disease, many of us think we have a built-in guidance system or guardian angel that will protect us personally from danger.

Therefore, on the one hand, we overwhelmingly agree with the statement "AIDS has made our generation more careful when it comes to sex," but we don't all behave that way in our own lives.

> AIDS hasn't really worried me, because, not having been single before, I feel that I have not been exposed myself. I am not at risk.
> Now that I am single, I think that I would choose my partner certainly carefully. I would be very careful about casual sex, but it doesn't enter into my thoughts a great deal. That may be a little risky, but that's the way it is.
> *Barbara, cashier*

> I was with a woman the other night. When I went to put on a condom, she got angry with me, saying it was a sign I didn't trust her. And, I thought, this is nuts.
> *Dave, teacher*

On the whole, we are being more careful. We can put it down to aging, the fact that most of us are married or in a relationship and that we are just plain smarter.

> Everybody that I know who is around my age group, around forty years old, has just made the decision not to fuck around anymore. I know more people who have fallen in love and are getting married.
> *Walter, tool and die maker*

> I wouldn't do it as frequently or with as many dif-
> ferent people now. I think AIDS is in the back of my
> mind. I'm not on birth control pills now or any-
> thing. That's usually my excuse for wanting to use
> something like a condom.
> *Leslie, ecologist*

> Disease certainly makes you think twice about
> extra-marital stuff and all that. I have thought of
> AIDS quite often as the new war. People don't real-
> ize there is a war unless it affects them. It's just like
> any other war. Like Vietnam, a lot of people didn't
> really know about it unless their high school friend
> got killed   Oh yeah, then it was real.
> *Benjamin, photo developer*

We would be naive if we didn't step back from this new morality to look at history. Syphilis was a major killer until modern antibiotics brought it under control. Gonorrhea was rampant, resulting in blindness, sterilization, and death, but millions contracted it even though they were aware of the risk. AIDS is not the first and will not be the last killer sexual disease. There will always be those of us who want sex with more than one partner.

As long as issues of trust, romance, sexual taboos, and fidelity are all knotted together, there will be casual, spontaneous, unprotected sex.

My own awareness of AIDS reads like a chronology from our generation.

The first time I heard of this new sexual disease was in an article in *Rolling Stone* magazine about a new, sexually contagious cancer. It appeared so far-fetched to me that I filed it in the back of my mind and ignored it. Bit by bit, during the early 1980s, word got out that a sexually fatal disease was hitting the gay community. No one was quite sure how it was contracted, but it was clear that it had to do with sex. Government was ignoring it because the Reagan administration was pathologically homophobic, believing that homosexuals were sinners who would be punished by God.

By the mid-1980s, the fundamentalists were on the bandwagon, pointing to a killer sexual disease that now had a name — AIDS. Like all good preachers, they knew that making sex bad and ugly was the quickest way to put a fish-hook into the soul. At this time, it was becoming increasingly clear that AIDS was moving out of the gay population into the heterosexual population. Yet, I still couldn't believe it. I didn't want the sexual revolution to end, and this sounded like its death knell.

By 1988, it was impossible to ignore aids. The U.S. surgeon general was recommending condoms; the fanatical right-wingers were trying to prevent any sexual education. Major magazines started printing long lists of brilliant, talented, compassionate people who had died of AIDS. The networks began creating AIDS docudramas. I knew it had hit middle America. I didn't know that it was going to hit closer to home.

In late 1989, one of my best friends, a creative partner I had worked with for more than ten years, told me he had AIDS. We held each other, cried, and didn't dwell on the horror to come.

During the next six months, I watched John die from AIDS, slowly, painfully, visited by appalling twists and turns as his immune system gave up the ghost. John died a few months after his forty-second birthday with as much dignity as he could muster even to the final day.

This disease will not go away. It is already rampant in Africa, Southeast Asia, and North America. We can fight it by practicing safe sex, funding AIDS research, and getting off our moralistic high horse.

AIDS is a terrible disease that is often transmitted by unprotected sex. This does not make sex a terrible thing. At all costs, we must avoid confusing the two. Sex is healthy, fun, and a source of great pleasure. Let's not lose sight of that.

Keep Love Alive

Nature's original plan for sex was simple — procreation, new human beings. For most of us, procreation is a very small part of our sex life. But once we do have children, everything changes, including our sex life.

During the first couple of years, exhaustion reduces frequency. We are so tired from getting up six times during the night that nothing else gets up either. As the child grows, a lot of necessary, mundane day-to-day tasks conspire to chip away at the spark and excitement of romance.

Compounding the problem, children make it harder to have spontaneous sex, drain a forty-year-old's energy, and refocus the relationship away from two-ness and toward the child.

On the whole, if you are married, forty, and have children, you feel pretty good about it. But you have to make sure that it doesn't interfere with the romance and the sex.

> Keeping a relationship viable takes work. It's just something you can't take for granted. Especially when a kid enters the picture, your values and priorities really change. You have to be very conscious of making time for yourselves as a couple without the kid. Not at his expense but to make things better.
> *Gordon, electronics repair*

Like it or not, we should take a page from all those magazines that tell us how to improve our sex life and marriage, and get to work at it.

> Although I was fairly promiscuous when I was single, I have come to see that you can have a strong sexual relationship with one person and have it play a pretty healthy role in your relationship.
> *Russell, consultant*

But most of us are like Russell. We have made our peace with monogamy and sexuality.

We like sex. We are more comfortable with our needs than we ever were before. We are healthier than any generation that preceded us. We are trying to be prudent when it comes to disease.

One final note on the changes at forty. Every man has occasional periods of impotence. At age forty, you have one chance in five of having difficulty getting an erection for more than five consecutive weeks. But, in nearly every case, the problem goes away when we relieve stress.

The odds are strong that sex will get even better with time. Even if it does get a bit less frequent.

Sex is fun. It leads to families. And families are an essential concern at forty.

Family

We Are Family

My ten-year-old nephew Brandon set me straight on the modern family. "I have four beds, you know," he said proudly. Then he proceeded to rhyme them off. One at home, one at his grandparents', one at our house, and one at the babysitter's. This ten-year-old nomad is an extreme example of the amazing changes that have taken place within our generation.

Brandon's father is a single dad who works shifts at a factory. He wants to keep his son and raise him in a stable home. But he doesn't have the money for full-time live-in help, daycare, and everything else it would take. So he relies on his parents, his sister and brother-in-law, and a friend who acts as babysitter when all else fails.

The amazing thing is that Brandon thinks this is fine. He enjoys the opportunity to go from one place to another and doesn't feel strange. After all, many of his friends live similar lives, bouncing back and forth between separated parents, spending more time at daycare than with their parents, rewriting the definition of the modern family.

Whatever happened to Jim and Margaret Anderson from "Father Knows Best" or Ozzie and Harriet Nelson? Where are those cosy Norman Rockwell images that we were supposed to be living at midlife? Why didn't anyone warn us it would turn out this way?

Instead of cozy nuclear families with a working father, a stay-at-home mother who bakes pies, two kids (a boy and a girl), and a friendly dog, all living in a house in the suburbs, our families are created in bits and pieces.

The bits and pieces are results of reorganizations through death, divorce, separation, and remarriage. The "blended" family is more common than ever before. The blend is children from two marriages thrown together and asked to create one happy family. The bits and pieces create problems.

Is the stepfather called "Dad" or "Jim"? Who is the real grandmother, and who is the slight outsider? Is there really a wicked stepmother? Are the bits and pieces in modern families creating latter-day Cinderellas? At forty, the answers are not so clear.

We are hamstrung by some of the more unfortunate fall-out from the 1960s. It involves the concept of what is "natural."

During the late 1960s and all through the '70s, we gravitated toward everything "natural." We wanted natural foods, natural water, and a natural environment. Natural living became the watchword of our generation. An underground comic, "Mr. Natural," experienced a brief, faddish popularity. Our search for the natural was a systemic reaction against change.

By the mid-1970s, we had focused on many of the negative side-effects of change, including the dangers of pesticides, a monetary system running out of control, and the "unnatural" working life that forced us to spend hours of each day trapped in a car. The solution appeared to be simple — revert to everything natural. Naturally, it was more complicated than that.

However, something else got caught up in the "natural" landslide — the family. And nowhere was there more damage done than in the search for "natural" parents.

As a reaction against change, we tried to simplify by saying that if something wasn't natural, we didn't want it. This led many adopted children on futile and heartbreaking searches for their "natural" parents. The sperm and the ovum suddenly took precedence over years of kind parenting, compassion, love, and consideration.

The wedge of "natural" was driven into new families created by the remarriage of parents, each with their own children. "Natural" seemed like such a simple way of telling the good guys from the bad guys. Of course, it wasn't. The issue continues to generate controversy, whether through surrogate motherhood or questions of custody.

But, finally, we are settling in with an acknowledgment that families today that are created by bits and pieces can be just as healthy, or more healthy, than those that follow an unbroken line from marriage through procreation to childbirth. And no matter how things change, we will continue to form families.

In spite of all the bits and pieces, all the changed rules and relationships, there is a natural drive toward coupling, toward creating a family, with or without children. Like salmon swimming furiously upstream against incredible odds, we keep our heads down regardless of the turbulence and keep moving toward creating family units, no matter how strange they may look to our parents. That is the family at forty.

The difference between our generation and our parents' rests in our willingness to recognize when something isn't working, to cut our emotional losses and try again. Our parents wanted to save face, to pretend to their Eisenhower world that everything was perfect. Perfect was defined as a husband who worked, a wife who stayed home and slavishly waited on her husband, raising children and doing what she was told. Like Canada geese, mates were expected to stay together for life and put silly notions of personal growth out of their heads.

We couldn't buy that. As children of change, we could survive only by adapting and growing. To us, this meant looking out for ourselves.

The word "growth" had limited meanings when we were growing up. It referred to something in the garden or the pencil marks on the wall measuring the number of inches taller we were than last year. The idea that a person could grow or change was restricted to a bunch of pointy-head intellectuals and antisocial types. As recently as the 1960s, the American Psychiatric Association suggested that a woman who wanted to go out to work, who wasn't content to stay home and wait on her husband, was not sufficiently "feminine" and therefore suspect in the area of mental health. What incredible hogwash! No wonder we rejected it.

> It was like my parents could never understand.
> Sure, I wanted to make them happy, but I really

couldn't see ending up like Mom, bringing Dad his
beer while he watched the game. So, I tried something different.

I lived with a guy, which drove them crazy, but
it didn't work out, so we split. I even got married
to make them happy, but he was such a jerk, he
was like my dad. So, now I am thirty-nine years
old and I'm not worried. I know who I am. I like
me. I don't need a date on Saturday night. Something will work out.
Lynn, university researcher

We want to be true to ourselves. We want individuality. Yet, we are
constantly coupling and creating family-style units, even if it takes us a
couple of tries to get it right. Or even if it doesn't look like the conventional family unit of old.

I Don't Like to Sleep Alone

At forty, most of us live with someone. Barely 9 percent of us live totally
alone, and more than half of us live in households with three or more
people.

The new family is a sometimes bewildering jumble of statistics.

For example, 9 percent of women who have no husband have a child
or other relative living with them. Of men at forty, only 3 percent who
have no wife have a child or other relative living with them. Three times
as many women as men are taking care of a child or relative at forty.

My son is the hardest part. His father and I are
divorced, so I have to wait for support and help
from him but he is slow paying, and sometimes I
think he's trying to hurt me through my son, but
he doesn't understand that it's hurting the boy and
it's his kid too.
Sheila, poultry processor

Most of us just don't want to live alone. It is cheaper for people to live together because there is only one rent, and many other expenses are shared. It also provides companionship. And, we have carried baggage from our teenage years about how it is normal and healthy to be married. So, we rush into marriage without always thinking about the consequences.

Marry Me

I have been married twice and before that I lived with a woman for two years, although I really didn't count it as a marriage. Two of these relationships had one thing in common. I went into them uncomfortable with the commitment, the compromise of sharing living space and the awareness that I had to account for my movements all the time. Even in my current, happy marriage these issues create friction from time to time.

By now, it has become a midlife cliché that men try to avoid commitment, preferring to stay free and loose. *Cosmopolitan* runs a cover virtually every other month that says "How to Get Your Man (Really!) to Commit." They then proceed to list the stratagems that have worked all through history, including making him jealous, threatening to leave, getting pregnant (an old-fashioned idea, except among movie stars), and performing his favorite sexual tricks.

There have been so many books written on this subject that it's not worth documenting here, except to say that things appear better these days. Even though men are less likely than women to want to rush into marriage, at least men talk about it now, explore it in magazines and on talk shows, and try to understand why we avoid racing to the chapel of love.

> Yes, I've thought about it a lot. The first time I got married was because she was moving to another city and I would lose her if we didn't go together. I didn't really want to marry, but it was the only way.
> Funny, we got divorced and I never thought I would marry again, but here I am getting ready to

walk up the aisle one more time.

At least this time, Betty and I have talked about what kind of space we need. How I need at least a couple of nights a week just for myself, and how she needs to know I'm not screwing around. But it's better than the first time I was married because I can talk about it and I don't feel like she's going to have a fit every time we come to issues of my independence.

Reg, social worker

These days, marriage is back in style — in part because people are deciding to have children and in part because the thrill of sexual experimentation of the 1960s and '70s is starting to wear thin. Also, AIDS is scaring people into marriage. Unfortunately, being scared into marriage is the same as being socially forced into it. The consequences of this social pressure during the 1950s were sexual frustration, resentment, bitterness, and divorce twenty years later. Being scared is the worst reason in the world to tie the knot.

During the 1960s and '70s, our parents tore their hair out because they thought we would never marry. Instead, we experimented by living together in what politely used to be called a "trial" marriage. But we knew better. We wanted sex and companionship without the formal commitment. And it worked out fine as long as our possessions consisted of a stereo, a bean bag chair, and three orange crates used as bookcases. But once materialism reared its ugly head, especially in the form of a family home, marriage became an all-important way to secure property. This ugly truth is fully realized during divorces.

During a divorce, people seldom talk about how much they are hurt, what they have learned from a failed marriage, or what they will do with this knowledge. Instead, they squabble about the family home, who bought the silverware, and who put whom through school.

Yet, in spite of trial marriages, questions about commitment, and the bomb craters of divorce, we still get married.

At forty, nearly 90 percent of us have been married at least once. And close to 20 percent have been married a second or even a third time. In other words, tradition has won out over experimentation. At midlife, we want more security.

Not surprisingly, there are more divorced and separated women than men out there — almost twice as many. It is easier for men to remarry. In spite of women's liberation, men carry more financial clout than women. They are paid more than women. They have more opportunities to earn money because they aren't spending as much time taking care of children. Also, many men do not want to take on the responsibility of more children in a new marriage. It all adds up to the fact that women get the short end of the stick.

Not everyone chooses to marry. About 10 percent of forty-year-olds have never been married. Most of these unmarrieds have made a sexual choice, gravitating toward gay or lesbian communities. A few simply haven't met the right person. And an outspoken minority simply like living alone.

> You know, sometimes I really get pissed off by people telling me I should grow up and get married. I am grown up. I have made a clear choice to live by myself. I like it. I have a lot of friends, men and women; I like my job; I enjoy time alone; I don't want to share a bathroom. What's wrong with that?
> *Tyrone, video cameraman*

For the past twenty years, the town criers have shouted that tradition and marriage are dead. The hysteria reached such a peak by the mid-1980s that it seemed as if every marriage would end in divorce, so there wasn't much point in even tying the knot. But the facts don't support this. If we dig beyond the sensationalism and gleeful finger-pointing that accompany most discussion of marriage among the Baby Boom, we find that the majority of men and women are married, and still in their first marriage, at forty. And those who aren't married are in a relationship.

Do You Want to Be Happy for the Rest of Your Life?

Since we have decided to stick together, how happy are we?

The good news is that the majority of us are happy, and a lucky third of us are "very happy" in our relationship. But almost 20 percent of forties surveyed are kind of getting along. The relationship is passable or unhappy.

At forty, we take stock of what we like and don't like in our life. In an ideal case, we decide to do something about it. But many of us who are trapped in unhappy relationships think we have to put up with them because "no one else would want me" or "there's nothing I can do about it" or "I've got to worry about the kids." All these excuses are destructive and ultimately do far more harm than good. All too often, we remain in relationships that aren't good for us because we feel guilty.

Fritz Perls, the brilliant healer and therapist, said that if we really want to understand our guilt, we should substitute the word "resentment" every time we use the words "guilt" or "guilty." Then we will know how we really feel. It is an important first step toward breaking free from a miserable life. I know. I have been there. Twice.

The first time I lived with a woman, I was in my early twenties. She was beautiful, unhappy, and screwed up. Very early in the relationship, my intuition bells were clanging and warning me away. But, like so many of us, I suppressed that early intuition and forged ahead. She wanted to live with me. I didn't have reciprocal feelings. Bit by bit, she began leaving things at my place — first, her hair curlers, then, some extra clothes. A few books followed, until, before I knew it, she had moved out on her roommate and moved in with me. As much as I liked her, I didn't really want her to move in. Why couldn't I say no?

Because I felt guilty (I did not learn to substitute the word *resentment* until close to my fortieth birthday). She seemed so confused and lost that it would be better if I put my needs aside and served hers. Of course, that is a recipe for disaster.

After a while, I couldn't stand it anymore and decided to move to another city, figuring that she would have to stay behind because she had one more year to finish at college. If I moved, I wouldn't have to tell her I didn't want to see her. Then, she wouldn't feel bad, and I wouldn't have to be the mean guy breaking up with her. Did I have a problem or what?

Much to my surprise, she transferred to a college in the new city and said she was coming along. I still didn't have the guts to say no. She followed me. I spent a miserable six months and finally got up the nerve to break the relationship. Two miserable years lost from my life because I didn't have the courage to stand up for what was important to me personally. That was my early twenties. Thank heaven, by forty I have learned that life is too short to stay in a relationship that is unhappy.

So, why do most of us get into relationships and then get married? The most common reasons are the desire for companionship, for economic security, to create a family, and for an outlet for regular sex. Oh yes, love is often cited as a primary reason.

Yet, if we look carefully at relationships and marriage, it is more likely that we fall into these patterns because of early conditioning in our life. Before we enter grade school, we are getting the marriage-and-family message. Little girls get toy stoves and dolls. Little boys get tanks. Although it may sound clichéd, the message is clear. Girls stay home and do the domestic work. Boys go out and fight battles.

By the time we are teenagers, our sex drive is socially channeled into "relationships." In other words, sex without a socially sanctioned coupling is a big no-no. Bit by bit, without knowing it, we are conditioned into the expectation that relationships in marriage are the only healthy way of living.

For millions of us who prefer to live alone, who don't feel a compelling need to couple up, society has only pity and scorn. At least "spinster" and "bachelor" have been replaced with "single," but the connotation remains. Unfortunately, many of us get into relationships because we think we should, rather than because we want to. The same is true for marriage. The same is true for having children.

Although there are millions of us who love children and want to have them around, there are millions who feel children are a burden, a difficult duty, and a terrible strain. And the subject is made even more difficult by the myths we grew up with.

Teach Your Children Right

The subject of children is clouded by historical misunderstanding, an attempt to be like our parents, and a blind obedience to outdated paternalistic thinking.

According to population experts, the "ideal" American family is an aberration that has happened only once in America history — right after the Second World War — and it spawned the Baby Boom. Our parents married younger than any generation in history and had children spaced closer together in more uniform numbers (two to four). Mistakenly, we believed that was normal.

If we had looked back and really studied our grandparents and grand aunts and uncles, we would have seen that one hundred years ago, they married later than our parents, that more than 20 percent of women never married, and that more than 20 percent of couples had no children.

Also, more couples had either one child or six, than two, three, or four. It is important to understand this historical perspective to put the following facts in the proper light.

At forty, 20 percent of us, or one in five, have no children.

For those who have children, the magic number is two — nearly 35 percent of forties have two children, around 17 percent have one child, and another 17 percent have three.

The number with no children goes up dramatically in cities with populations of more than 2 million, as well as among those forties who hold postgraduate degrees. In part, the population link is related to the fact that larger cities have higher concentrations of gays. On the educational side, it seems that we often put off having children while we get more education, only to find out that we've waited too long.

Children change our lives — particularly men's.

> Fifteen or twenty years ago, I didn't want to have a child. It was the last thing on my mind, and I looked upon it as a negative and an impediment to what I was doing.
>
> Funny, it was almost forced on me because it was, like, okay now's the time I've got to get married and that was only because of the pressure that I was going to lose the woman I loved if I didn't get married. So I was kind of dragged into marriage and fatherhood, and it worked out nicely.
> *Gary, screen writer*

A child is the first opportunity we get to provide and receive unconditional love. For some reason, most of us can't give unconditional love to our mate. We always find reasons — no matter how trivial — to be critical. But, with a child, we suspend this criticism for a while. The child loves us so unconditionally that it opens our hearts and reveals hidden places that we never knew existed.

This awareness of a love that has always been inside of us, triggered by a child, is so powerful that instead of marveling at how well we have hidden this enormous love from ourselves, we believe that the child is the only way we can get in touch with it. It is the reason that most of us have so much trouble letting go of children as they grow up. Equally important, a child gives us a chance to look back to our own childhood, to the forces that shaped us and made us who we are. More than anything, we don't want to replay the bad. We want to build on the good.

> Well, it is just a really neat thing, an indescribable thing. It is really cool to me to be somebody's Dad. And I found that I am kind of reliving my childhood in a way that I never could when I was growing up.
> I would say we were a poor family who were not privileged by any means, and there were a lot of things, physical things, that I longed for as a child that I could never have. Now my son fortunately can have them, . . . so, I can kind of relive my youth through his eyes. That is a really neat thing.
> *Patrick, dentist*

Yet, this is the age of fractured families. We marry; we divorce; sometimes, we remarry. As we do, the kids get shuffled around. The love gets misplaced or overlooked. More often than not, through desire and circumstance, it is far more often a single mother who raises a child than a single father. Among Baby Boomers, this adds up to more than 3 million children with a single parent in a relationship.

The long-term consequences for our generation are troubling.

The significant majority of these children are being raised by single mothers who are not receiving fair child support from the fathers or social support from the government.

We have a responsibility to help other forty-year-olds who are in this difficult position. If we can't find charity in our hearts to do it for them, then let us do it for the children. They are growing up in a difficult time.

The good news is that we will experiment with ways to help these parents and children. Already, a few enlightened businesses, often headed by Baby Boomers, are working to provide better, affordable daycare. Our artists, filmmakers, and writers will create new stories and myths to empower these children.

The runaway hit *Home Alone* was a huge success because its hero, a resourceful seven-year-old whose experiments helped him fend off the dangers of the adult world, provided comfort for millions of "latch-key" children. It is so easy in the movies. In real life, we will have to create healthy myths for children raised in a topsy-turvy world.

Some of us will be lucky because we will be able to get help from our parents. It is miraculous how much most parents change when they become grandparents. They try to make up for everything they think they did wrong. And it often endears them to us. But it doesn't take away the conflicting feelings we have about them.

Mom and Dad

There's an old joke that goes like this: When I was fifteen, I thought my parents didn't know anything. By the time I turned twenty-five, I was amazed at how much they had learned in ten years. At forty, we are amazed that there was ever a time when we thought they didn't know anything.

The good news about forty is that we get along better with our parents and siblings than we did at thirty, and we like them more than we did then.

> When I was twelve or thirteen years old I just got
> to the point that I felt like I had no use for my par-
> ents. I didn't need them in my life at all. And it is
> only since I have got a son of my own, who is six
> now, that I've come to realize how much my par-
> ents really did for me, and frankly how much I

love them. I feel that same way about my sister.

And up until recently, the last few years, I kind
of felt the only thing me and my sister had in common was that we were brother and sister. But now
the barriers that existed between my sister and me
have dissolved, and there's a closeness that's hard
to describe. It is sort of a family bond, and I think
it is really healthy and positive in that regard.
Joey, map maker

Why do we get along better with our parents? Are we smarter and
wiser? Are we just tired of the fight? Do we develop tolerance and
patience as we get older? Or is it simply the fact that, at forty, we are the
same age that they were when we were teenagers?

I like to believe that we get along with them better because we have
grown, because our spirit and our soul have opened to love and forgiveness. Sometimes, it is very hard to forgive parents who have been cruel,
insensitive, or abusive. The pain is so strong and the hurt runs so deep
that we can't let it go. But often, forty allows us to forgive without having
to put ourselves in danger.

Sometimes I just shake when I think about it. My
grandfather sexually abused me as a child, and I
know my mother knew but didn't stop him. For
years, I hated both of them.

Now, I have children, and my grandparents
want to see them. Finally, as a Christian, I have forgiven him. And I let him see the children. But
never alone. There's a big difference between forgiveness and stupidity.
Elizabeth, hotel concierge

We forgive our parents because we have come to understand our own
humanity more completely. We forgive our parents because, at age forty,
more than half of us have lost a parent, usually a father.

When a parent gets sick or dies, it really focuses the mind and forces
us to re-evaluate our relationship with our parents. In our teens, most of
us thought our parents didn't understand us. And we were right. We

were going through the incredible change and experimentation that characterized our youth, and intuitively, we knew they didn't really understand it. However, at one level, they did understand us. They just didn't know what to do about it. They had been young once, full of ping-pong hormones and confusion. They felt sorry that we were having to go through the same thing.

With benefit of hindsight, we start to mellow toward our parents. More often than not, we are likely to forgive our mother before we forgive our father.

Men in our fathers' generation got saddled with a hard role. They were the disciplinarians, the out-of-home workers who didn't have a lot of time with the children. All day long, the stay-at-home Moms were there to nurse wounds, read books, and bake pies. Dad got saddled with the role of heavy — "just wait till your father gets home."

Also, our fathers often did work they hated. Whether they worked in factories, mines, or a dehumanizing office, they felt as though they had to sacrifice to provide for a wife who couldn't work and for children who needed education. Inevitably, their resentment was subconsciously converted into blame for their wife and children. Although not universal, their problem was widespread enough to have permeated our consciousness.

> Fathers. There is this distance. There is a part of
> you that wants to go across that distance and then
> there is a part of you that maybe at forty says,
> "Fuck it, let him come across. I am tired." I want
> to be careful not to make that all sound negative
> because there are positive parts of fathers, but why
> are they so removed?
>
> And the relationship with my mother is more of
> someone that you can talk to. I grew up in a facto-
> ry town and went off to war, like my friends, in
> Vietnam. And I used to write home to her, all these
> long letters, telling her how I wanted to be an
> actor. And in my town that was the weirdest thing
> anybody could think about. But when I got out, I
> did it.

> And recently, I went home and sat with my
> mother and talked about my anger toward my
> father and she said, "How do you feel now that
> you are forty?" and I said, "I feel like I am going to
> do whatever I feel like doing."
> *John, actor*

For every man who has trouble with his father, there is a woman who has conflict with her mother. Most women have a secret dread of turning out like their mothers and, in spite of their best efforts, are horrified when they see the negative, critical traits that shaped them coming out in their treatment of their own children. Often, that is the point where courage meets commitment, and they break the subconscious re-enactment of the mothering they received.

For some reason, mothers have real difficulty understanding that their children have aged beyond seven or eight. No matter how much they acknowledge achievement, professional advancement, marriage, and aging, they have a mental lock on nurturing and babying. They changed enough diapers, soothed enough frayed nerves, and interceded with enough irate fathers to feel they earned the right to keep us young. But to grow, we have to get free from this.

> I have become a lot less tolerant of my mother's
> bullshit and criticisms because I thought, "I am
> almost a forty-year-old woman, not fifteen." I have
> a kind of indignation that she doesn't want to be or
> wasn't respectful of my adulthood. And I have less
> tolerance for not being treated as an adult by my
> family of origination.
> *Joanne, clinical psychologist*

At forty, it's a real struggle to put Mom and Dad in perspective. We love them out of a sense of duty, because they raised us and helped us get a start in the world. We love them because they loved us. We love them because there is no "because" to love.

But growing up is a process of separation. It starts when we physically leave our mother's womb, the separation of one body from another. It speeds up when we start to walk, putting greater physical space between ourselves and our parents. It hits high gear when we reach puberty and our sex hormones rev up. Nature is preparing us to have our own families, separating us from the one we are born into. It's true that the hardest part of love is letting go.

The difference between this generation and the previous generation is the fact that our parents are living longer and we are living longer. A generation ago, fathers were dead by age sixty-two and mothers didn't make seventy. There weren't a lot of forty-year-olds with living parents. Now, we have the opportunity to get to know our parents as real adults, past midlife, looking to them as harbingers of what is to come. Even if they try to keep us infantile, we can talk as adults, express ourselves as adults, and try hard to get them to listen.

At the same time, the fact that they are living longer will provide us with a problem that will take place on an unprecedented scale — caring for an aging population.

> I have become the parent to my dad in a lot of ways. He is still independent and self-sufficient, but he is getting old and his health is failing. He has hypoglycemia and glaucoma and has gone blind in one eye. Every little thing that happens, he feels he needs to call me and ask me what to do about it. If he lives another fifteen years, I don't know where it's all going to lead.
> *Elizabeth, assembler*

> I think it has really come full circle. My parents were really good to me when I was a child, and now at this particular stage in my life I'm taking care of them.
> I make sure my mother has her treats to eat because she's on a semi-limited diet, and I drive her around when she needs something. Sometimes, it gets very hard when I have other things to do, especially at work, but what can I say? They

took care of me when I was young. I'm taking care
of them when they are old.
Dwayne, sawmill operator

Right now, our parents are still young enough that they don't need constant care. But soon, we will be faced with very difficult decisions, ranging from whether to put them in nursing homes or have them come to live with us.

At eighty-two, my father is slightly older than the fathers of most forty-year-olds. Although he has emphysema, he gets around all right and really enjoys his life. He has always been a very active man, gardening, taking care of the house, and keeping himself on the move. Like most children, I didn't notice the changes in him because they happened slowly. Obviously, I've noticed the fact that he shrunk an inch and a half over the last ten years. He walks a little slower and can't hear as well. But, for some reason, I could never get it in my mind that he would ever stop being the man I knew him to be.

So, I was surprised when he told me recently that he was thinking of selling the house and moving into a condominium because taking care of a house was just too much for him. It didn't seem possible. Not my father. And then I realized that I was coming to an extremely difficult time in my life. How will I help my parents? As much as I love them, I'm not sure I could stand to have them live with me. I certainly don't want them to live in a nursing home. And we don't have enough money to give them full-time help.

I have been agonizing over what I see as an inevitable, excruciatingly difficult series of choices.

As I agonize, I keep coming back to the word "selfish." Oh, sure, I can rationalize things away by saying I didn't choose to be born into this world and therefore my parents had a responsibility to take care of me, but I don't have a responsibility to take care of them. But, that is rationalization. In my heart, I hurt.

For over a decade, I have been thinking about the word "selfish." The more I think about it, the more I talk to my friends, the more I realize that we have often been characterized as a "selfish" generation. We focus on ourselves.

Some old-fashioned thinkers calls this "narcissism" and say that we are a spoiled generation, whose self-centeredness will eventually be the downfall of the nation. They are going too far. They are also wrong.

Our "selfishness" has a very clear explanation. It is important to understand it as we get older.

I Want to Be Selfish

We are going to hear the word "selfish" a lot over the next decade because there are going to be so many painful family decisions that will pit the martyrs against the survivors.

Our parents are living longer on average than at any time in history — especially mothers. Who will care for them when they start to become older and more infirm? Will they move in with you, or will you put them in a home? If they don't want to go into a home, will you be selfish?

Cheryl Russell, author of 100 Predictions for the Baby Boom, says that the burden of taking care of aging mothers will fall on their daughters who are already burdened with raising children and taking care of a family. For many, the stress will be devastating. Will we suffer guilt, or will we be honest and say that our guilt is really resentment?

Many of us have already agonized through the guilt and resentment involved in divorce and child custody. If our emotional survival means getting out of a bad marriage and losing custody of children, what does it say about us as people? Is selfishness always the flip side of healthy growth? At forty, are we cursed with a no-win situation where our own personal feelings must always be consumed by others' needs?

For more than ten years, I have struggled with this question. And every time I think about it, I keep coming back to the self and selfishness.

For twenty years now, self-styled experts have made the "me generation" the conventional wisdom about the Baby Boom. It is a negative vision, and supports the outmoded and dangerous assumption that focus on the self is inherently bad.

If these "experts" looked at it from an objective angle, the behavior of the Baby Boom would make complete sense to them. The explanation is simple.

The Baby Boom has to focus on the self in order to survive.

No other generation in history grew up in a period of such rapid and continuous social and technological change. Affluence and mobility created a massive middle class that generated the highest levels of education in history.

Changes in communications, ranging from television to computers, have restructured the social and business landscape. The changes have been so striking that, when we looked for models and examples to help us adapt, we found them outdated and ineffective. We needed new models. As a result, we became experimenters.

We discovered that the only way to prosper and grow is to experiment constantly. We had to try new ways to deal with new problems, even if the experimentation was as "frivolous" as letting our hair grow long or as radical as "dropping out" from the mainstream.

While we experimented, we discovered something very important — the self. We realized that we had to look to the self rather than the family to survive and grow.

We didn't arrive at this discovery through ego or poor childrearing practices. We happened upon it while experimenting with change in an ever-changing world. A brief history will help clarify how this happened.

A few hundred years ago, most people didn't need to think much about the self. Their actions, hopes, and fears were all constrained by a social structure that pretty much told them who they were, what they could do, and where they could go. As long as they knew their relation to the king or ruler, to their peers, to their immediate bosses, and to their religion, it didn't matter if they knew anything else. When times got tough, it was these relationships that would determine their fate.

Within these structures lay the most important structure of all — the family. Even if the social structure failed them, people could fall back upon the family. The most important issues were still relations — the first-born son, the dutiful wife, the father as provider and head of the household. And as long as families stayed close together, this arrangement worked reasonably well. But families didn't stay together.

As the world changed, families grew farther and farther apart. Sons and daughters ended up thousands of miles from their mothers and fathers. Help was no longer close at hand. Simultaneously, another, more substantial, shift occurred.

Parents no longer knew more than their children. They couldn't even pretend they did. Knowledge was growing so fast that it was impossible to keep up. Specialization was a survival tool. Parents couldn't control or intimidate their children by using or withholding knowledge. Mass media gave anyone who could read or turn on the TV access to it all.

When Dad couldn't help with homework in the New Math and Mom couldn't accept that the birth control pill was being widely used by high school girls, the kids knew it was over. In reality, we had known for years.

We rolled our eyes when we heard our parents say, "Why, when I was a kid . . . ," because we knew it didn't matter. Anything our parents knew as children was obsolete.

As this awareness grew, we knew we couldn't rely on the old ideas and the old wisdom to power us through an ever-changing world. Intuitively, we knew that if we couldn't rely on the family, we would have to rely on the self. To rely on the self, we would have to understand it better.

So, our hypereducated Baby Boom embarked on another experiment — learning about the self.

We talked about self, read about self, and dreamed about self. We rejuvenated Jung and Freud. We experimented with drugs to probe the inner reaches of the self. We explored psychology, mysticism, and biology — all in search of the practical focus on self.

We learned about our needs, about the mechanisms that make us tick, about what we want from life. We began the painful and difficult process of unraveling our parents' influences and needs from our own. As we learned more about ourselves, it became more important to keep ourselves healthy than to pander to the unhealthy demands and needs of those around us.

Our parents took the brunt of the blame for our problems. "They screwed us up" . . . "They didn't know what we needed" . . . "They were insensitive to our childhood pain" — and on and on and on.

Luckily, most of us have come to our senses at forty. We realize that most parents did the best they knew how at the time. Yes, there were alcoholic, sadistic, insensitive parents who never wanted children. But the majority tried. And most of us get along better with our parents than we did ten years ago. We want to like them again and ask them questions about our own childhood. It is a comforting relationship.

But the real test will come when our fully realized self is called upon to care for an aging parent or parents, when it conflicts strongly with our own personal needs.

Most of us will rise to the challenge. It will be difficult, painful, and expensive. It will strain our personal resources, and we will look to government to provide more help. This is a special irony because we forties have convinced ourselves that we need less government rather than more. As the shit starts to hit the fan, we are going to reconsider that idea.

Strange Magic

A family is two or more people who choose to live together. Usually, it is sanctified by marriage, but that isn't always necessary. Most families include children.

But a lot of us put off having a child while we added more education or climbed the corporate ladder. We ignored biology, thinking that willpower and determination could somehow make anything happen. Instead, we are finding that we may never have children.

> I have a lot of girlfriends who are kind of tragic. They are in their late thirties and not married, and are terribly depressed.
>
> The thing that has broken their hearts is that they haven't found the man of their dreams. And the thing that has broken their hearts is that they want to have children and don't think they ever will. One had endometriosis and the other has lupus, and they are pretty seriously sick.
>
> And they have made strange compromises. One of them has moved back in with her mother and her sister who is divorced so that she can take care of their fresh new babies, and in that way she will have babies in her life. The other one works in an

adoption agency, trying to place kids who might
not have a chance. It's strange how they both have
children but never had children.
Cheryl, car rental clerk

That is why I am optimistic about the family at forty. We may not have traditional families, but we have growing, experimenting families. We are trying out new social configurations that will work in our mobile, global village. Experimentation always involves risk — the chance of pain and the opportunity for great breakthroughs. So far, we have experimented with marriage and children. Although some children have been hurt by the rupture in families, they have also learned that the world goes on, even if only one parent is there. They have also learned that it is better to be with a parent who cares than with one who doesn't.

The next hurdle is our aging parents. Once again, we will have to experiment. Will we put them in nursing homes? Will we form communes for our aging progenitors? Will we generate a rash of home renovation that includes an extra apartment in the basement or added to the back of the house so that a surviving parent can come to live with us? Although the answers are unclear, we will keep experimenting until we find something that works.

The good news is that we live in an age of massive communication. If someone finds a way to deal with a portion of the problem in Wyoming, it will be picked up in magazines and we can read about it in Arlington. If an experiment in Seattle produces good results, it will end up in TV documentaries within a short period of time. We will communicate.

And that is the next stop on the journey at forty — communication and what it has done for us, how it has shaped us, and what it holds in our future. For me, communication made a quantum leap around the time I first heard the Beatles.

The Beatles

You Really Got a Hold on Me

My sister tied me to a chair and sold me to her girlfriend so that she could see the Beatles in concert.

I didn't like being tied to the chair, and I wasn't crazy about her girlfriend, but it seemed the only way to get the hottest ticket in town in 1964. And she promised to take me along.

Tickets were pricy, ranging from $3 for the worst seats in the house to $6 for front row center. They were impossible to get, the show having sold out a few hours after it was announced to 15,000 crazed fans, eager for a chance to see their idols.

I don't remember the date with her girlfriend. I remember the concert.

We had the worst seats in the house, so high up that you needed oxygen tanks to breathe. Luckily, I brought binoculars so that I could see my heroes in the flesh. Even though I could see them, I could barely hear because the screams started a few minutes before the Beatles walked on stage and stopped long after they'd left. Coupled with the strobe effect of thousands of simultaneous flashbulb pops, it was my first major media experience. And I was hooked.

I had never felt such energy in my life. It was as if I had been lifted up on the screams, surfing a thundering wall of hysteria on a ride without end. This was it — freedom, rebellion, sexuality, and hope. Impossible as it may seem, the tinny p.a. system, simple floodlights, and long-distance view hooked the rock 'n' roll junkie in me. From that moment on, I was a child of the media.

Like millions of us, I started with a transistor radio, got a cheap record player (for 45s), and graduated to a small, portable *stereo*. As for TV, I persuaded my parents to buy a gizmo called the Roter so that our outside antenna could pick up more stations. I saved my money to catch such acts as Roy Orbison and Little Eva after school. I bought records — singles and albums — listened to music whenever possible.

I tried to join a band but couldn't sing in tune, so I became a manager. It was a short-lived and humbling experience.

As I grew older, I wanted all the media toys — stereo television, a VCR, a compact disc player, a big-screen TV. And every grownup kid's toy — Nintendo.

Sometimes I think my media toys are attempts to recapture the innocent magic of early rock 'n' roll. Or, possibly, I am using my toys the way media guru Marshall McLuhan described them — to extend my senses in every way I can. And although the early days are blurring, I still feel that the Beatles started it all.

Another Girl

Looking back over my relationship with the Beatles, I still feel the vitality and wider creative horizons they gave me. But if I am going to be honest, I have to admit that my original interest in the band sprang from baser motives — unrequited love and a touch of lust. It began with a high school crush.

She was beautiful and intelligent, and lived close to my house. She was interested in hockey players, football players, and everything else I wasn't. She liked me as a friend, and I kept hoping for something more.

One day, she shattered my world by telling me her father had been transferred to Scotland, and she was leaving soon. We quickly agreed to write regularly.

Within a few months, she was writing back that she was crazy about a band called the Beatles. She had pictures of some guy called Paul splattered all over her wall, and asked me if I had heard about the group.

Although this was only thirty years ago, in terms of communications it may as well have been the Dark Ages. No one I knew had heard of the Beatles. This was October 1962.

I began going to record stores and asking about this band that was stealing the affections of my unrequited love. Who were they? How had they captured her so completely? She had never shown this kind of interest in any of the "Bobbys" — Bobby Darren, Bobby Vee, Bobby Rydell. She hadn't even seemed interested in Elvis, and didn't bat an eyelash when he went into the army. Yet, here she was, writing long letters, mooning over a band called the Beatles, whom she had just seen live in some club near Glasgow. I wouldn't rest until I had heard their music, condemned it, and told her so.

Finally, my persistence paid off. A record store owner told me that a new band from England had just put out an album called *Meet the Beatles* I bought it right away, took it home, and my life changed. Instead of writing to Scotland about how bad this band was, I joined the fan club. Soon, we were writing back and forth every week with our feelings about the Beatles. After that, things moved fast. Within a few weeks I heard the band was to be on Jack Parr's show, and I ran all the way home from the pool hall (the Billiard Academy, as it was officially called) to see them on TV. I was blown away. I played the album for my friends, and most of them thought it was some of the most exciting music they had heard in a long time.

To put this in perspective, when Elvis went into the army, music had hit a real low. Other than "The Twist" and a few novelty songs, radio was churning out safe, bland, pleasant songs such as "Take Good Care of My Baby" and "Volare." It was so boring that "The Twist" became a number-one song during two consecutive years, proof that there wasn't much new in the music world. The Beatles led the revolution that knocked down the safe, middle-of-the-road music that had been passing for rock 'n' roll.

My Beatlemania continued unabated. When I saw them live in concert I was hooked for life. I began to grow my hair longer, facing down friends and high school vice-principals who thought it was too revolutionary.

Twist and Shout

I loved the Beatles. They changed my life artistically and personally, providing a symbol of freedom, rebellion, and the power to live creatively. They were young, irreverent, talented, and unmistakably foreign.

Not all my friends felt the same way. Many of them thought the Beatles were dandies, poseurs who used the gimmick of long hair to cover up their musical limitations. These friends favored the Rolling Stones.

Also, there was a big group who simply didn't get it. This group was composed of crewcut guys who associated long hair with juvenile delinquents; pony-tailed girls who still thought Elvis was dreamy; and older brothers and sisters who were into jazz, the Four Aces, or country music and who saw the Beatles as a threat to everything they held dear. They were right.

The Beatles were about to change our way of looking at the world. When Bob Dylan sang "The Times They Are A-Changin'" he needn't have looked farther than the Beatles for the symbol of change. Long hair became the symbol that thumbed noses at conformity and the old way of doing things. It's amazing to think of the tidal wave that started with about half an inch of extra hair.

In retrospect, it's funny to look back at what was considered long hair on the Beatles. It was nothing more than hair combed down across the forehead and hanging ever so slightly over the ears. Later, by the time they recorded *Rubber Soul*, the Beatles' long hair was really long, down to their shoulders. So, why did it create such a stir in the first place?

The Beatles' hair was the first major break with the almost Japanese-like conformity of the Eisenhower years. The 1950s were the era of the organization man, the conformist, the people who just tried to fit in. Our parents.

They had lived through a Depression where individuality was quickly squelched in pursuit of any available job. That was followed by a war where the individual had to set aside any free expression to fight in a uniform army — short haircut, the same clothes, the same look.

When the war ended, the industrial manufacturing mentality ran on unchecked. It said that the best worker was a conformist, someone who did what he or she was told, dressed as he or she was told, and pushed all the right buttons. During the 1950s, this was translated into a look that included short hair for men, bobs for women, conservative clothes, and a numbing conformity that generated a ferocious backlash beginning in the 1960s and lasting well into the 1970s.

By 1963, short hair, neat clothes, and fitting in were the name of the game. Then, John Kennedy was killed. The man who had refused to wear a hat at his inauguration, the man who symbolized youth, hope, and aspiration, was gunned down.

After the requisite period of mourning, we needed a party, something to celebrate, a way to cut loose. The Beatles arrived to fill the bill. We moved quickly, not only throwing out hats but growing longer hair to replace them. It was a simple act of rebellion that any teenager could perform without spending money, time, or even effort.

Long hair said, "We are different. We can take charge of our own lives. Nothing is ever going to be the same."

It was a stroke of incredible good fortune that the Beatles were not only style-setters but revolutionary and evolutionary musicians.

The Beatles threw down the creative gauntlet, challenging visual styles, musical tradition, and the role of the rock star. Instead of mumbling polite answers to journalists' questions, as Elvis had, they were witty, irreverent, and very clever. They became a media circus.

Revolution

The Beatles changed so many things — our hairstyles, our musical horizons, our way of looking at life.

To me, they were always creative big brothers, just one step ahead, leading me into expressions, sounds, and ideas that were challenging yet somehow familiar. But, no matter how big the Beatles were, they were part of something much larger — a media revolution.

The media revolution was and continues to be a communications revolution. Portability and miniaturization are the twin levers guiding this change.

When television burst on the scene in the mid-1950s, it quickly adopted all of radio's content, including variety shows, dramas, and even Saturday-night bandstands. In order to survive, some radio owners hit upon the radical notion of playing favorite songs over and over. Coincidentally, the biggest baby boom in the country's history wanted to hear these songs. And Top 40 radio was there to provide it.

The Beatles and Top 40 AM radio were made for each other. And the timing was just right.

When the Beatles invaded, Top 40 radio had already permeated the country. There were at least one, and often two, Top 40 stations in each city aimed exclusively at audiences under the age of twenty. If these stations played a record, everybody heard it at the same time. It was played over and over again until we learned all the lyrics, got tired of it, and waited for the next release. Often, our mothers listened to the radio with us, keeping in touch with what we were doing and learning the same songs. It was a unique period in media history, never to be repeated.

By the early 1970s, AM radio was afraid to play the experimental, ground-breaking music of the Beatles, the Rolling Stones, Led Zeppelin, Cream, and Jimi Hendrix. Wedded to the idea that songs on radio had to be shorter than three minutes and have comprehensible lyrics, Top 40 AM radio began a slow but steady decline. Simultaneously, thousands of new FM radio stations came on the scene across the country, fragmenting musical sources and forever de-massifying rock 'n' roll. But for ten brief years, between 1963 and 1973, we all heard the same songs at the same time, and they became part of our life.

> I remember the first time I heard the Beatles on the radio. One morning my clock radio went off and "I Want to Hold Your Hand" came on. And that song was so unique, like something I'd never heard before, and it was electrifying.
>
> And the next thing I knew I was talking to my friends who were saying "Have you heard about this group, the Beatles?" and they were saying, "Oh, man, aren't they unbelievable?" We were all talking about them.
> *Dirk, merchant marine*

We heard them on the radio. There was something fresh and seemingly innocent. More than anything, they gave us hope.

I remember sitting doing homework in Grade 9
when "She Loves You" first came on the radio with
my little transistor sitting on my desk and that was
a great revelation. I remember leaping around the
room when I heard that final chord with the four-
part harmony and just feeling so much and thinking, "God, there's hope, there's people out there
who are this successful already, who feel this way
and can express it so well."
Martha, computer operator

Think for Yourself

Not everybody loved the Beatles. Shortly after they began electrifying
our generation, a backlash started.

In the beginning, it was innocent enough, pitting the Beatles against
the Dave Clark Five. Remember them? Back in 1964 and '65, a few misguided souls said they liked the Dave Clark Five more than the Beatles.
But that was mere posturing. The serious split came with the advent of
the Rolling Stones.

The Stones were dirty, blues-rooted, and authentic. They had no
Nehru jackets, ties, or clean hair. Instead of singing love songs that
ended with a kiss, theirs ended with a slap in the face. Suddenly, the
Beatles were too clean cut, too polite. The Stones were real. And it
seemed to cut across class lines.

In my home town, there was a kind of class structure around the Beatles and Stones that could
loosely be related to the Mods and Rockers. Where
I came from there were rich kids and then blue-
collar kids. Although my parents were working
their way up and had little money, I was still a
blue-collar kid. Our society was broken down
completely by music.

The richer, whiter kids listened to the Beatles
and the Beach Boys, and myself and my parents

listened to the Stones and the Animals. Old blues
music.
Richard, actor

In the beginning, the Beatles symbolized light and hope. The Stones
symbolized darkness and anger. It seemed like such a long way from the
Beatles' "She Loves You" to the Stones' "Under My Thumb." But if we
looked carefully, the distance wasn't very great.

Rather, the Beatles drew from a wide range of musical sources,
including Broadway musicals, American rhythm and blues, country
music, and even skiffle music, a popular form in Britain. The Stones dug
deep into blues and rhythm and blues, seeking their inspiration in music
designed to numb pain.

For a while, as teenagers, we felt compelled to pick one band instead
of the other. But, within a few years, the Beatles and the Stones were
singing about the same thing. Mick Jagger couldn't get any satisfaction
and John Lennon was crying for help. By this time, the Beatles and
Stones were part of a larger polarization — the revolutionaries against
the status quo.

The revolutionaries lined up behind the Beatles, Stones, Doors, Bob
Dylan, and the Jefferson Airplane. They wanted to change the world —
to stop war, pain, and dishonesty and create a world that was fairer,
more humane, and more fun. Although there were a few bomb carriers
in the group, the revolution didn't center on blowing up buildings.
Rather, its focus was the destruction of the walls of the status quo, especially an old-fashioned, hierarchical, deferred-gratification way of thinking. Marijuana reorganized these walls for many. LSD melted them for a
few. It was like a New Year's Day that lasted for years — out with the old
and in with the new. It had been a long time coming.

It's easy to forget that during this confusing revolution, millions of
Boomers didn't want things to change. More than 30 percent of all forty-
year-olds say the Beatles were not at all important to them or that they
were a negative experience personally. There was a lot of threat in people
who spoke with an accent, dressed funny, and had long hair. Forty-year-
olds who live in small towns, make less than $30,000 a year, or have
only grade school education are most likely to feel negative about them.
But millions more embraced the change that revolved around these

remarkable musical geniuses. By the time the Beatles sang about Revolution, it was already well under way.

> I really liked the idea of combing my hair down in my face, but I didn't grow it long until about 1966 because high school rules were really strict against that. The more radical British groups like the Stones and Kinks annoyed my parents, and that was great too. It helped in establishing a personal generation gap.
>
> But, in the beginning, the Beatles weren't much. They were fairly acceptable to a lot of parents because they were so cuddly, cute, and witty. In my school, the Beatles became a girls' group. In a way, it was my little sister's group until *Revolver*, maybe *Rubber Soul*, even *Help!* actually. When they started maturing a little, things changed.
> *Ken, rock critic*

In the beginning, a lot of parents and even kids wrote the Beatles off as a gimmick. Revolution was still a radical, threatening concept. Millions of parents disagreed with Dr. Spock, preferring to believe that the best child was an obedient one with no mind of its own. For many, it was hard to accept the revolutionary messages that were coming through. But, in the long run, we kids had to rebel because separating our own needs from those of our parents was an indispensable part of growing up.

> In the beginning, I didn't like the Beatles much.
>
> I was brought up in a real strict Catholic family and the Beatles to me was like talking about Hitler. But then I listened, and the more I listened to their music and my mother heard it, the madder she got and the more I wanted to listen to it. I listened to the words of the songs and listened to their meanings and bit by bit I realized that they were saying something very important to me, and my mother

really didn't know anything about my life.
Anne, medical sales

Rock 'n' roll music challenged the status quo. We accepted that and began to change our lives. It created conflict, tension, and change. Some of the change was healthy. Some was not.

The Beatles themselves went through the same crises, challenging the world and finally one another. Their individuality overpowered their need to stay together as a group. And they dissolved as a band.

By the time the Beatles broke up, their messages of love, anger, hope, and the human spirit had broadened their appeal so much that they became symbols to a generation. As our awareness grew, their relevance increased proportionately.

> The more I was aware of what was happening in the world, the more their music seemed to parallel this and have a message to it. I think there was something divine about it. That their music in a sense was trying to give us the way to go.
> *Elsa, waitress*

Sergeant Pepper's Lonely Hearts Club Band

If the Beatles started a fashion revolution with long hair, they started a bigger musical revolution with their landmark album *Sgt. Pepper's Lonely Hearts Club Band.*

By the time this record came out, the Beatles were bigger than life. Their films were huge successes. Their music was everywhere. But they still weren't taken "seriously" by most people. *Sgt. Pepper* changed that. It was such a landmark that everyone sat up and took notice. It signaled that rock was now "serious" music.

The album was played in music schools and debated on the pages of *The New York Times* and even in high school classrooms.

For me, the record was a vindication of my unabashed Beatle worship, which had started even before I was tied to the chair in the garden and sold to my sister's girlfriend for a date.

I never felt particularly rebellious as a teenager, but I always felt that the postwar Eisenhower world was dull, constrictive, and deadening to the soul. Even before I could articulate my feelings, I knew something was wrong. For me, music was a way to open my soul, to find words that expressed my confusion, passion, longing, and hope. It was the poetry of my emotions. And the Beatles were my poets laureate.

I bought every Beatle album within a day or so of its release and played them over and over again, always being amazed by the fact that the band seemed to be just one step ahead of me musically, socially, and spiritually. But no matter how much I admired them or followed them, I wasn't prepared for *Sgt. Pepper*.

Strangely enough, I first heard *Sgt. Pepper* on AM radio in Miami. By the time the album was released, the Beatles were such big news that many radio stations sent disc jockeys to England to pick up a copy of the album before it was released in the United States. They premiered it with enormous fanfare, capitalizing on the fact that the Beatles were larger than life.

Even on an AM radio station, the music was radically different, revolutionary, and creatively exceptional. I couldn't wait to buy the album.

When I bought *Sgt. Pepper* a week later, another surprise lay in store for me. It included a lyric sheet! This was wonderful. Instead of having to listen to a song fifteen or twenty times to figure out the lyrics, I could get into it right away. It was poetry and music combined.

Sgt. Pepper was the culmination of the Beatles' experimentation with drugs, religion, technological recording techniques, and their own growth toward adulthood. It was so different from anything that had happened in rock music before that it challenged listeners to expand themselves when they listened to the music. One of the most popular ways to do this was to experiment with marijuana or psychedelic drugs such as mescaline and LSD.

Sgt. Pepper completed the transformation of our generation from clean-cut, obedient kids to experimenters who seriously questioned the status quo. And it all happened so fast.

In 1964, hardly anyone had long hair, marijuana was a "bad" drug associated with Beatniks, and no one in their right mind would want to induce schizophrenia chemically. Just over four years later, long hair was the new status quo, drug experimentation was spreading faster than a brush fire, and parents everywhere were confronted by strangers they used to call their children.

Although *Sgt. Pepper* didn't cause the change, it provided the necessary symbol to our generation. It said that experimentation could produce greatness, that music was the handmaiden of growth, and that we were entering a new world for which we had never been prepared.

We went into the new world gladly, like children, not afraid of the unknown but excited by the possibility of adventure. If the Beatles could experiment, so could we. If music was the siren call to growth, then let the music play.

Suddenly, artists were recording on eight-track tape, mixing complex orchestral sounds with rock. An artistic and technological revolution had begun.

Here, There, and Everywhere

When *Sgt. Pepper* hit the scene, it was a technological tour de force. At that time, there were no recording studios with tape recorders that could lay down eight tracks side by side so that they could be mixed the way they are today. These days, portable recording studios in a teenager's basement often have twenty-four tracks.

When *Sgt. Pepper* arrived, most people were lucky to have a stereo record player and an FM radio. A few adventurous souls had reel-to-reel tape recorders for high-quality sound. Television stations broadcast in a mix of black and white and color, depending on the time of day and the show.

There were no Sony Walkmans, no big-screen or stereo TVS, no in-home VCRS, no Dolby sound at movie theaters, and very few FM car radios. As for cellular phones in cars . . . well, that was as much science fiction as Dick Tracy's two-way wrist radio.

During the past twenty years, we have come to take portability and miniaturization for granted. What would life be without a Sony Walkman when we jog? It's hard to imagine the days before remote-control television with a mute button or the VCR to watch those movies we'd always planned to see.

At forty, we no longer have to wait for a disc jockey to bring a record on a plane from England so that we can hear it on am radio. If we really want to, we can use a fiber-optic phone line or a satellite up-link and hear recording-studio quality anywhere in the world at the same time. We have access to so much information and entertainment that we are overwhelmed. Often, we don't know how to keep up because there is so much going on. Information overload dogs our waking, and a few of our sleeping, hours. There is so much happening in the world of entertainment that an entire daily news show, "Entertainment Tonight," is scheduled after the "real" news across the country. How do we handle all of this at forty?

In part, we retreat into the past.

We listen to our old favorites. We replace old records and tapes with compact discs of the same songs. We take comfort in familiarity, in the musical messages that helped shape, reaffirm, and ennoble us.

> I can chronologically formulate my life according to the different Beatle albums and when they were released.
>
> For example, I know that when their *White Album* came out I was working at a factory for Chrysler. I remember taking an enormous amount of time cleaning this car which I had carefully booked time to clean because I knew the radio station was playing the album in its entirety. So I got a Lincoln Imperial with the best stereo of that time in the car and spent my entire lunch hour preparing the car for the dealer while listening to the Beatles. No one ever got a cleaner car.
>
> Then when *Magical Mystery Tour* came out I had my first encounter with marijuana. *Rubber Soul* was a dark album to me because it was a dark time in my life, and *Abbey Road* was a really uplifting period with friends getting married and life being great.
>
> *Doug, lumber salesman*

As we retreat into the past, watching "The Wonder Years" and TV specials about the 1960s, we do it with very modern equipment. At forty, more than 90 percent of us have TVs and VCRs. Most of us have cable television and some kind of Walkman-type tape unit. However, very few of us own big-screen TVs, video cameras, or cellular telephones. We spend our money on music and television programs.

Twenty years ago, we would have been astonished at the idea that we could pop down to the local store on a Saturday night and rent a movie for $2.00, uncensored, uninterrupted with commercials, to be viewed as often as we like. We love to rent videos; nearly every forty-year-old surveyed had rented at least one during the last month.

The Beatles ushered in this musical and technological revolution. Since then, technology has turned our homes into entertainment centers, revolving around the television, remote-control channel changer, and VCR. We have stopped lying in our beanbag chairs, listening to new records through king-size speakers, preferring the easier ride with television.

And we suffer Video Guilt. Video Guilt sets in when it's time to tape a show on TV and we realize that all our video cassettes are full. But we haven't watched half the shows yet! Trying to decide which show to record over before we've even watched it gives us Video Guilt. But we shouldn't feel bad, because 64 percent of everything recorded to be watched on a VCR never gets seen. It is recorded over before it gets a single viewing.

Top of the Pops

It was more than twenty years ago today that *Sgt. Pepper* told the band to play. Now that we have all this perspective, what can we make of it? Do we still have favorite artists? Have things changed with time?

I asked forty-year-olds to name their top-three favorite musical artists of all time. The Beatles topped the list, beating the next two contenders, Elvis and the Rolling Stones, by almost two to one.

Top-Three Favorite Musical Artists of All Time

| | Men | Women |
	%	%
The Beatles	24	23
Rolling Stones	17	4
Elvis	5	15

The Long and Winding Road

When I first heard the Beatles, I was a Paul fan. He was good looking, and didn't have the moody menace of John Lennon. Yet, over the years, I realized that John's songs touched me the deepest. "In My Life," "Strawberry Fields," "Help!," "A Day in the Life," and "Imagine" transformed me powerfully.

As I grew older, I realized that I shared a lot in common with John Lennon. I had been a very angry young man, covering my unacknowledged rage with wit, charm, and an unwillingness to commit to jobs, women, or anything that might tie me down.

As John Lennon struggled with his growth through LSD hallucinations, the meditations of the Maharishi, and machinations of Yoko, he represented a struggling, loving spirit unfolding. His road was painful, disorienting, and challenging, but it pointed toward goodness and growth. Increasingly, I looked to him as an inspiration, the kind of man who could disentangle from his demons and grow.

I compared him to Mick Jagger, a great musical talent, but a man who looked the same as he did twenty years earlier, as if nothing had changed in his life. By contrast, John Lennon, who was changing, experimenting, and growing, often suffered derision and contempt from fans and the press alike. But he stayed true to his growth.

In his music, I was inspired by "Imagine," one of the most beautiful songs for Utopia in modern times.

At one point, John took a five-year retreat from the world to raise his son, and returned with poetic, powerful music such as "Starting Over" and "Woman," reflecting a new sensitivity to himself, the people around him, and the world. At age forty, John Lennon was an inspiration to me about what forty could be. I had just turned thirty.

The day before John's death, I was in New York, working with *Rolling Stone* magazine publisher Jann Wenner. He showed me a Polaroid photo of John and Yoko lying naked on a bed, and told me he would put it on the cover of *Rolling Stone* in a couple of weeks. I was shocked and upset.

Even though I knew John was being true to himself, I knew this would further alienate his fans. But I admired him for his authenticity.

That night, I went to a Broadway play and dropped over to a friend's for a visit afterwards. As I walked into his apartment, I heard Beatle music, on the radio, and Nick looked up at me and said, "Have you heard? John Lennon's been shot." I was stunned, horrified, and despondent. It wasn't just the end of the Beatles; it was the end of my role model, the man who would help me be forty.

My hotel was a few blocks from The Dakota, where John was shot. By the time I got there, kids from New Jersey were driving up the street, hanging out the windows of their car, shouting "Which way to The Dakota?" The next morning, the city was unnaturally quiet. For the first time in my life I saw businessmen my age and slightly older walking quietly along the street, formally dressed in suits and heavy overcoats, with tears running down their cheeks.

I was crying too.

To me, John Lennon had always seemed like an older brother whom I admired from a distance. Somehow, I connected emotionally with him and transferred my fan mentality into a spiritual bonding with his pain and growth.

Through his music, writings, and interviews, I developed a picture of a man who tortured himself and others while struggling to break through to a higher spiritual plane. His suffering was expressed with exquisite artistic realization in songs such as "Strawberry Fields," "Help!," and "In My Life." His lyrics touched me and moved me, helping me get closer to my own pain, need, and anger. Although they were always one-way conversations, I felt like I was talking with my older, wiser brother who had to do everything the hard way so that it was easier for me to learn.

After his five-year hiatus from recording, I was thrilled when he came back with a song entitled "Starting Over." It symbolized the fact that pain, suffering, and despair could be transformed into growth, love, and a second chance. My older brother had shown me the way.

When he was shot, I felt as if someone had torn my belly out. I have lived with that pain and loss ever since. It may sound irrational and a little desperate to put so much stock in a man I never met, but it shows the power of the Beatles, John Lennon, and the music.

Imagine

With John Lennon dead, I wondered how I would ever understand forty, fifty, or even sixty. I had hoped that he could artistically and spiritually show me the way.

In the months following his death, I realized that it was essential to make the most out of every moment in life. Death could come in a heartbeat. When it did, I wanted to know that I had been true to my own beliefs and what was right and important for me.

It took me almost ten years to put John Lennon's death and age forty into the same frame of reference. He had been killed close to his fortieth birthday, just when his life was starting over. His watchword was "imagine." It is the word that can free us to do great things at any age.

Imagination is the most powerful tool of mankind. When we imagine, we set the wheels of creativity and greatness in motion. It took imagination to believe that we could fly. Until we imagined it, no one would commit the resources or technology to making it come true. The same imagination is required to imagine a cleaner world, safer cities, a cure for AIDS, or the end of war. Imagination alone can't solve problems, but it sets the creative process moving toward positive change.

When we are little children, we are full of wild and fabulous imaginings. We imagine monsters, dragons, Santa Claus, and the Easter Bunny. Somewhere along the line, schools and our parents start to kick the imagination out of us until we check our imagination with phrases such as "that might be nice but it's not practical" or "that's not the way the real world works." As our imagination is drained out of us, we lose energy and we get old.

Yet, at forty, it's essential that we rekindle the imagination, that we recognize the possibility of doing more with our lives and the world around us than we once thought possible. If we recapture the optimism of the 1960s, which imagined fairness, racial equality, and a world at peace, we can imagine a better life for each individual self. At forty, we have the power to do something about the job we don't like, a strained relation with our parents, or even the house in which we live. If we turn off the TV for just one evening and imagine the world we want for ourselves — imagine it in detail — we can do something about it and make the second half of our life so much better than the first.

John Lennon never got a chance to take his imagination all the way. During his five years of introspection and withdrawal from the world, he was just getting started. For many of us, his death was the first major celebrity death that hit us personally. It forced us to grow up, to consider the end of something that mattered. It forced us to ask all sorts of questions that began "What if . . ." — "What if John had lived and the Beatles had got back together?" or "What if gun control laws had been in force before his assassin bought a gun?" It brought us face to face with re-evaluation of the past. And this re-evaluation is one of the most difficult challenges of forty. It is our regrets.

Regrets

Regrets, I've Had a Few

Sometimes, when I'm tired, overworked, or just plain down, I get torn up by regrets. As my defenses go down, my self-pity goes up and I start with the "if onlys," my long list of regrets. Once I get rolling, I can run up a pretty long list of things I wish I had done differently during my life. But when my defenses get back up and I'm feeling good, I can just brush regrets off. When I brush them off, I can convince myself that there is no use looking back and getting hung up on something that can't be changed.

More often than not, I find myself bouncing back and forth between the "if onlys" and the "so whats." On the one hand, I find reconciliation by telling myself I can learn from my regrets. On the other hand, I can't suppress the frustration or self-criticism that tells me I really could have done something different. I seem to spend my time trying to make peace between the two extremes. I call them Zen and un-Zen.

As a child of the 1960s, I am often tempted to take the Zen approach. In this one, I have no regrets. Everything that happened, happened for a reason. My growth, my present happiness, could have come about only with the broken relationships, wasted time, poorly focused goals, and misadventures of my youth. That's Zen.

But sometimes I don't feel very Zen-like. At those times, I regret my undergraduate college education, which disappeared while I played cards and stayed up until 4:00 in the morning. I regret many relationships I entered for the wrong reasons and stayed in too long. I regret . . . At about this point, I begin to adopt the Zen approach again and realize that if I hadn't gone through all those regrettable adventures, I wouldn't be writing this book.

No matter how much I intellectualize it, I have one big regret — that I didn't stand up earlier in life for what was important to me. Instead, I was easily manipulated by others whose emotional needs always seemed more pressing than my own.

Early in life, I had learned to keep a stiff upper lip, repress my real feelings, and cater to others. I became expert at figuring out people's moods and feelings, and then trying to help them. If they were depressed, I was a natural comedian. If they needed a shoulder to cry on, mine was always there. It was so ridiculous that in high school I lent my homework to friends who were too lazy to do their own. I was always there fulfilling other people's needs.

This early pattern got me in trouble as I got older. People took advantage of me, and I knew it. But for some reason I couldn't stand up to them, tell them what I needed, what was important to me. The result was a series of bad relationships in which I constantly felt frustrated and unhappy. Finally, after several years of positive therapy, I broke through and got control of my life. Ever since, it has been great — most of the time.

Looking back with the clarity of hindsight, I regret that I hadn't learned about myself earlier, that my life couldn't have been happier before this. Since misery loves company, I'm glad I'm not alone with my regret about failed personal relationships: It is the one that tops the list for forty-year-olds' number-one regrets. If only we could undo the bad marriage, the hurt that the kids suffered, the divorce. If only.

I asked forty-year-olds, "What is your number-one regret in life?" The list looks like this.

Number-One Regret at Age Forty

	Males %	Females %
Problems with personal relationships	28	38
Not enough education	16	19
Bad career choices	12	10
No regrets	10	10
Money/financial	9	8
Health	4	5

What can we make of this list? What can we do about it at forty?

Regret # 1: End of the Innocence

The biggest regret of most forties is relationships gone wrong. Marrying too early, marrying too late. Raising our children the wrong way. Never marrying. Not having kids. The death of a spouse or close relative. Our regrets with relationships are a dance of contradictions.

Some of us wish we had more relationships, more sexual encounters. Others regret a pattern of lifelong infidelities and one-night stands.

There is more regret around marriage than anything else. The wrong kind of marriage. Marrying too early, marrying the wrong person. One woman in ten says that a bad marriage is her biggest regret in life.

Ironically, for every woman who regrets remaining married too long, there is another who regrets never marrying.

> I regret that I didn't get married ten years ago. But, unfortunately, the person I was going out with was already married at the time. It was just a shame because it would have been quite good. I wish that at this point in my life I had two or three kids and could go on from there.
> *Iris, translator*

It is a kind of a "damned if you do, damned if you don't" scenario. If we spend all our life waiting for the right person, it's possible he or she will never come along and we will be left without a spouse. On the other hand, if we jump at the first person who comes along, as so many of us do when we're young, we can pay an enormous price for the security. We lose the chance to grow, to become the person we know we are. Instead, we are trampled down in a bad marriage, wishing we had made another choice.

Regret is a two-sided blade. No matter which side you touch, you get cut. Even if we make the right choice in a marriage, we can still find something to regret, such as the timing.

> I wish I would have waited a little longer to get
> married. Maybe till I was thirty. Materialistically, it
> was very hard. In the last four or five years we
> have finally had anything to speak of. Up to that
> point it was all hand-me-down furniture.
> *Luis, meat packer*

Timing. It's another side of regret. It's the clock that ticks when we say "if only."

It is easier to have regrets about timing than almost anything else. How often have we said "If only I had met you at a different time" or "The time is not right for having children"? Yet, it is this very decision around children that can be the most powerful regret of all.

There are women who think their timing was off by being too soon — that kids arrived too early, making it hard to be a good mother. But, for every forty-year-old woman who said she had kids too early and wasn't a good mother, there were two who wished they had more children or had had them earlier. In other words, when we look back from forty, more of us regret what we didn't have — children — than what we did have.

Even when we have children, we can regret the fact that we don't have enough time to spend with them, or to be good parents. For every woman who said she didn't put enough time into parenting or spend enough time with the kids, there were two men who felt the same way. Time had run away with their lives.

As we get older, we become so much more conscious of time. Three minutes was an eternity in grade school. It's the blink of an eye at forty. A year was a lifetime when we were thirteen. It seems only a moment at middle age.

In our twenties, we are likely to stay in relationships much longer than we should. We are always looking for the change, the good news that everything is finally going to work out, the light at the end of the tunnel. It doesn't come and we accept it or we move on. At forty, there is a heightened urgency, a sense that each year is more precious, each moment of wasted time a greater loss. We really get the urge to make changes.

> I have a regret for staying in relationships with women longer than I should have, which is probably something both sexes could attest to. I still see it all around me at work.
>
> You know, my secretary says, "I've been living with this guy for seven years, I don't know if we're going to get married or what" and I say, "Hey, wake up and smell the roses!
>
> "You ain't getting married, you're wasting your time. Take six months off, fall back, drink, listen to blues records and then go out and life's going to be wonderful."
>
> I know this because I allowed myself to get dragged down in a couple of relationships that started out great but when they got bad I was reluctant to cut the cord. That's a regret.
> *Leon, manager*

Inevitably, when the subject turns to love, marriage, men and women, there are regrets about children.

In previous generations, most regrets about children focused on having too many, having children too young, or having insufficient means to make their life comfortable. Couples often felt they had lost a chance for personal happiness because they were burdened with too many children too early in their lives.

For a small number of forties, this is still a big regret. However, our generation is the first to experience widespread regret about putting off children until midlife.

Frankly, I regret not having children sooner and earlier in my life. And at least at this point in time, I regret not having more. But I feel like I am still not over the hill and there's a possibility for children in the future.
Bruno, welder

When it comes to marriage, my regret is that I wanted ten children. But I'm thirty-nine, not married and I just don't know. I mean, could I really hustle if I started now?
Tanya, modeling agent

Once in a while, we are faced with terribly difficult choices when we are not ready to deal with them. When young, we often adopt a cavalier attitude toward responsibility, especially sexual responsibility, and end up facing the consequences later in life as we replay the old tapes and suffer strong regret.

I find myself saying to myself I'm awfully serious these days. And people tell me that too. I know that as a young man I was much lighter-hearted and goofy and crazy. I laughed a lot and made jokes. But I think that changed around the time I was involved with my carelessness around sex.

First, there was the abortion. Later, I gave up a child. I think that had a deep moral and emotional effect on me.

It's been hard, but I think that I've forgiven myself and amazingly, twenty years later, I met the woman again and we had an emotional affair. Even though she is married, we went over all those emotional scenes, and I feel a lot of it has been absolved. But I just don't laugh at jokes as much as I used to.
Geoff, editor

Relationships are the core of human civilization. When they are positive, supportive, and enjoyable, they enrich our lives and make them complete. When they are fractured, discordant, and out of sync, they leave us empty, angry, and lost.

For a brief but heady part of my adult life, in my mid-twenties, I tried to avoid relationships with women. Instead, I just wanted to have fun — to go to parties, to have sex, to enjoy conversation, and avoid commitment. No matter how much I tried to do this, women had an almost primeval instinct to push for a more formal, structured relationship.

The word "relationship" always seemed to be a synonym for "fence." I never got the impression that relationship was a dynamic give and take. Instead, it seemed to be a set of rules that put limits on freedom and what was permissible. The rules might be little things, such as "We have a relationship if we go out every Saturday night together" or "We have a relationship if we see each other at least twice a week." Relationships didn't get defined by what we could do but rather what we couldn't do. As a result, I began to think that "relationship" meant suffocation.

Yet, in spite of my forebodings, I kept getting drawn into "relationships." With the hindsight of age forty, I realize that I was drawn in because I couldn't stand up for my own needs and my own feelings. Unfortunately, the more I gave in to someone whose needs were out of sync with my own, the more resentment I felt.

In my un-Zen state, I truly regret that I couldn't learn about healthy relationships without an enormous amount of pain. Sometimes, I still regret what happened to me, even though I learned so much that I am healthier and happier now.

I got involved with a woman who didn't like herself. On the surface, she seemed very together. She was intelligent, attractive, and a great conversationalist. Yet, from the first moment we met, my alarm bells rang and told me to leave. Another part of me shut the bells off. It is the part I regret. The part that tries to make other people happy at the expense of my own needs.

The whole relationship revolved around her neediness. She needed me to live with her so she could feel better about herself. So I did. Not surprisingly, nothing much improved. Then, she needed me to marry her so she could feel better about herself. Reluctantly, oblivious to my own needs, I put on the ring. Things got worse.

During this time, she tried suicide — several times. After talking to her therapists and friends, reading every book I could find on the subject of depression, and working through my own therapy, I came to a simple conclusion: Some people don't want to live. Life is too painful for them. And nothing we say or do will change it. It will merely postpone the inevitable.

After several years of marriage, I suddenly realized that I was in a living hell that I had created for myself. I had to get out. And I did. But not without belly-deep pain, body-wracking tears, and seemingly endless accusations and recriminations. What a mess.

I regret it. I wish it had never had to happen. But, putting on my Zen hat, I see that it did have to happen. It taught me enough so that I could marry my current wife, Pat, and be happy with her. And it was part of the process that led to writing this book.

Regret # 2: Don't Know Much about History, Don't Know Much Geography

Our parents always told us that if we went to school and got an education we would have a better life than they had had. The martyrs among them were quick to point out that they were suffering so that we could get an education and have the life they never did.

Obviously, the martyrs struck a chord. Almost one in five forties has a regret about education, most wishing they had more schooling. But a remarkable, small group wish they had never gone on to university.

> Education . . . that's the other regret I have. I regret
> having spent so many years in university. I think I
> was sold as a young man from a middle-income
> family that the benefits of education were great.
>
> But I just feel that I could have been working. I
> could have been involved in the real life of my
> chosen field of music and learned that way.
>
> Now I find that I could have pursued my love
> of music and learned as much and probably gotten
> more contacts in the business. I'm sorry about that.

> All that generation, where I came from, was taught
> that university was the way to do things.
> *Lorne, choreographer*

Regrets about too much schooling are focused on the fact that some careers and jobs grow with experience. The sooner you get started, the better you get.

> I regret going to college. If I had stayed in Los
> Angeles instead of going away to school and start-
> ed writing when I was seventeen, I would have had
> a major jump.
> *Jennifer, script assistant*

However, most education regrets come from missed opportunities, chances not taken, doors left closed.

> When I was a junior in high school, I was chosen
> to study in Spain for a semester and my dad made
> a kind of disgusted face and I thought we couldn't
> afford it, which was baloney, 'cause we could, I
> know now. And I would have gone and studied.
> I've always kind of regretted that.
> *Ida, gerontologist*

By and large, education regrets are simply the issue of not getting a degree.

> I regret that I never got my college education. I
> really regret that because these days people won't
> even read your résumé unless you have a four-year
> degree. That is what they try to emphasize.
> *Doreen, quality control inspector*

In our chop-and-change society, degrees are a shortcut that let employers narrow the field before they start interviews. There is an assumption that a degree guarantees certain basics such as the ability to read, write, and think. Unfortunately, in many cases, an undergraduate college degree carries the same weight that a high school diploma did thirty years ago. It promises little more than a very basic level of competence.

These days, with complex, sophisticated business ringing the globe, postgraduate education is increasingly important. And many of us are spending another four years getting a law degree or an MBA to help us get that all-important job. But, I can understand regrets about the wrong kind of schooling.

Sometimes, I regret my undergraduate education. My parents always wanted me to be an actuary — an insurance statistician who bets on when you are going to die — because it paid really well. When I graduated high school, I knew I didn't want to be an actuary but couldn't think of what else to do, so I compromised and did a degree in economics. I hated economics. I thought economists were way off base, and I almost had a nervous breakdown.

After graduating, I took a couple of stabs at working at economics but hated it so much that I quit both times after about eight months. Then I decided to do what I had always wanted to do — study with media guru Marshall McLuhan.

It meant that I had to go back and take nine extra undergraduate courses to get into the University of Toronto in the Masters program. I did them at night school and summer school, and finally went back and did a whole extra year as an undergraduate. I went into the Masters program with no hope for a job when I graduated. I simply went to study what made me happy. It was the best move I ever could have made.

I won a scholarship to study for a Ph.D., took part-time work in advertising and marketing, and set the stage for my future career without even knowing it. But I still wish I could get back the four years I lost studying something I didn't like.

Regret # 3: Where Should I Go?

Hindsight is regret's powerful searchlight. It illuminates the corners where we took wrong turns; it shines on paths we might have taken. It blinds us to the fact that it is so much easier to look back than to look forward.

In hindsight, many of us regret that we spent our lives in the wrong job or working too hard. Career regrets center around a lack of clear goals, the wrong job, working too hard, or not being employed in a field we want.

When we are working toward a goal, our focus on the end result helps us to forget the difficulty and discomfort of getting there. When we achieve the goal, we ask ourselves what we really have. That is the dilemma of forty.

We set out after money, thinking it will bring us happiness. When we have the money and no happiness we realize we should have set out looking for happiness instead. We set out looking for a move up the social ladder, thinking it will bring us peace of mind. When we move up the social ladder, we seldom have more peace of mind. With hindsight, we realize we should have set out looking for peace of mind.

At forty, with hindsight, we realize that setting the right goals is the key to the puzzle.

> I would definitely say I should have taken the business side of the career more seriously. Sometimes I think that if I'd really planned it right and had great financial planning and good business sense, it probably would have put me in a better position right now.
>
> My major regret is not doing what I've done recently in taking charge of my career. It's been poor career evolution. I wasn't taking risks when I should have. Sort of chickened out. I shouldn't have waited eight years to say I've got to get out of this job that I hate and get into something I like.
> *Don, convenience store manager*

There's not a lot to say about hindsight. It's easy to guess where we went wrong.

The challenge is to act on it, do something positive, recognize that the wisdom gained at forty is a tool that can't be bought with money. We can all use wisdom to make sure the second half of our lives isn't punctuated with the same regrets about relationships, jobs, paths not taken, and a lack of relevant goals.

Regret # 4: No Regrets at All

How is it possible to have no regrets? Surely all of us have something we regret? But one in ten forties says he or she has no regrets. Maybe he or she is wearing the Zen hat.

The regret-free can't be psychopaths with no conscience. There couldn't be that many of them. Rather, they are the mere 10 percent of us who have got their act together. They have accepted life as it comes. They have let regrets go.

> Sure, there are things I might have done a different way, or situations that got out of line. But what's the use of getting upset about them? It's not like thinking about it will change them or make me a better person. So, I learn. It makes a difference.
>
> I guess when you asked me that, whether I have regrets, the first thing that came into my mind was, "There's no point in crying over something you can't change."
> *Hector, real estate agent*

Regret # 5: Money, Money

For most forties, money isn't the biggest regret. It's far down the list for people who make more than $30,000 a year.

A few of us regret not being rich and not getting to do the things we wanted to do because of a lack of money. Almost the same number regret not having bought a house earlier or wish they had a larger home. But, at forty, we have learned that money isn't everything. We know that we can do something about our life at this age and earn money.

> At times like this, I can kick myself. I just never thought it through. We should have bought a house fifteen years ago rather than keep putting it off. We should have invested instead of spending.

If I could do it over, I would. I'm not sure what I
would change but I know I would change something.
Adrian, forklift operator

Regret # 6: If I'd Known I Was Going to Live This Long, I Would Have Taken Better Care of Myself

There's nothing like a fortieth birthday to focus the mind on health.
There's a sharp appreciation of the fact that we no longer have the energy, stamina, or elasticity we had twenty years ago.

Forty is a kind of inventory: a physical stock-taking; an examination
to see what needs replenishing, reworking, or reshaping.

Most of our health regrets concern bad habits.

I regret that I smoke cigarettes and I want to give it
up. Put that in the book. I am going to quit.
Christopher, jewelry salesman

I would have never taken drugs. If I knew then
what I know now, I would never have smoked pot
and would never have drank a lot. Because what
happened to me I think happened to a lot of people. I went through ten years of malaise. I could
have realized all the dreams that I had when I was
in my teens and my early twenties if I had never
gotten involved in drugs.
Susie, travel agent

Regrets about drugs such as alcohol, cigarettes, and other mood-alter-
ing substances are outpaced by the biggest health regret of all — too
much weight and not enough exercise.

I used to work out and feel great. Then I met my
current boyfriend and we both stopped going to
our fitness clubs and joined a tennis club instead.

And I remember thinking at the time that this was
great: "I'm loved, I don't have to worry about this
exercise stuff. I can just let myself be what I want
to be and not sweat so much." And I stopped exercising, and that is a regret I have for sure.
Arlene, writer

That's Just the Way It Is

At forty, most of us realize that life did not turn out the way we visual-
ized it. This type of regret can really tear us down, get into the psyche,
and paralyze us. It's essential that we acknowledge regrets and let them
go. Otherwise there can be no growth.

What I regret is when I was seventeen I never
expected my life to be this way. I always expected I
would be married by the time I was twenty-three,
have two kids, become a writer, have a lovely man
in my life and everything would be settled. It
would just all be settled. I'd be moving somewhere
forward.

And when I was at Berkeley recently, parked
outside, I just had this wave of nostalgia. It just
went shuddering over me and I burst out crying. I
just said, "I just wish it could have been the way I
thought it would have been." And it wasn't and it
never will be.

Every now and then in the past two decades
I've had twinges of how come it isn't like I thought
it would be. I've obviously made choices which
have made it the way it is, but the dream never
died, the dream never went away. Somewhere, I
just thought things would fit into place, and they
didn't.
Anita, designer

Anita doesn't really understand that she was manipulated by the same myth that most of us were fed when we were young. It said that for a woman, marriage, children, and a man automatically fit all the pieces into life. The myth promised a painless, stress-free form of growth. With hindsight, we know that can never be. But the myth is powerful and deep. Many of us carry regrets for destructive myths that were never realized. It takes a lot of work to pull out a hook that has been sunk that deep.

Regrets can become overwhelming if we let them. But they are nothing compared to the thinking we will have to give religion as we age. If regrets are looking back, religion is looking forward. Regrets are a useful tool to make sense of an earlier time in our life, to correct destructive behavior and to make positive change. Religion requires our focus on the end of life, our spirit and soul.

There is no better time to evaluate heaven and hell than age forty.

Heaven and Hell

It's Over

The weirdest part of turning forty is the increasing certainty that we really will die one day. We can put it off, but it is inevitable.

If you are forty, there's a 50/50 chance that one of your parents is already dead. You know death can come.

During the past few years, you or someone close to you has been so sick that death seemed near. There's nothing like a really severe flu to provide a shocking reminder of mortality. It comes on fast, quickly debilitates the system, and provides a fevered reminder of our tenuous grasp on life.

Now, this could be depressing stuff. If there's one thing that we don't like to think about after our teens, it is death. As teenagers, we are preoccupied with death, weighing the pros and cons of suicide, wondering whether life is worth living, and feeling powerless because we don't think we can do anything about it. As we leave our teens, we get some control over our world. We gain education, job experience, and a new set of friends. Eventually, we marry, start a family, and put thoughts of death behind us. Once we have responsibilities, we can't afford to die. We can't even entertain the notion.

When we take the time to think about death, we are puzzled and frightened by its finality. It is especially frightening at forty, just as we are starting to make sense of life, figuring out how we can really enjoy the rest of it. The thought flashes through the mind — What happens if I suddenly die? What will I have made of this life? The "what" is so powerful that all major religions give us another chance at life.

Christianity and Islam give us an afterlife: a stress-free holiday in the hereafter for the good ones, a vacation nightmare for the bad ones. Hindus and Buddhists believe in reincarnation, which gives life again in a new body. With reincarnation, we get our heaven or hell on earth.

No matter where we place our heavens and our hells, we are faced with one unavoidable fact: Most of us don't agree with each other's beliefs.

You May Be Right

When it comes to an afterlife, most of us can't agree on the form it will take. Christians, with their intense belief in eternal salvation or damnation, are at odds with a larger majority of the world's Buddhists and Hindus, who believe in reincarnation. In the Middle East, Christians and Muslims kill each other over religion. Hindus and Muslims kill each other too.

Even among Christians, wars have been fought and lives lost over disagreements on how to interpret the Bible. All in the name of the same God! In Ireland, Catholics and Protestants murder each other, weighing in mightily with religious justification. In the Middle East, warring factions of Islam fight each other, then wheel suddenly, unite, and attack Jews.

Often, this religious ping-pong is naked ambition and greed cloaked in piety. It is a trick that has worked for thousands of years, so it is no surprise that it is still in use today.

But beyond the ambition and hypocrisy, there is outright fear. Every religion tells us it is the only one that will work. There can be no other. One is right and everyone else is wrong. How do we choose in that environment? And once we have chosen, would we be willing to change again?

> I have a heck of a problem being sure about reli-
> gion. I have met enough smart people who believe
> different things from me that it sometimes leaves
> me confused.
>
> But since I don't know which one is better than
> the other, maybe it's best to stick with the one I
> was raised with and try and make something work
> from that. I mean, what if I changed and I picked
> the wrong one?
> *Ernie, feed lot operator*

Most of us, when faced with uncertainty, stick with habit and the decision we have already made. So, it's not surprising that most of us haven't changed religions. More than 90 percent of forty-year-olds surveyed haven't changed their religion during the past ten years.

But habit doesn't explain why barely half of us believe there's a real heaven or hell and why most of us are not frequent attenders of church services.

Those explanations lie in the modern world, which has shaped a unique group of forties.

Just a Little Rain

We were born in the vast shadow cast by the smoke from Hiroshima and Auschwitz. The world had been strained by the Great Depression, which was followed by a global war of astonishing scope.

Our parents were thrown willy-nilly into this new order. Fathers traveled to foreign countries and saw more horror than they ever imagined possible. Mothers worked on the war effort at home, suffering loneliness, deprivation, and fear.

Shortly after the war ended, a new Cold War began, a vicious psychological guerrilla game played for planet Earth. In this game, the rules permitted atomic weapons — lethal killing devices that would wipe out hundreds of millions of people and poison the earth for a thousand years to come. The scale was so vast and the stakes so high that it challenged all our old assumptions about right and wrong.

How could God allow this?

That is the sort of weighty philosophical question that has kept theologians busy for thousands of years. Until recently, they could point to the fact that we understood so little about our world that we simply had to rely on faith. There was God and Satan; there was faith. That was the end of it.

Modern science messed all this up. On the one hand, it experimented relentlessly to demystify our world. On the other hand, it concocted a witch's brew of chemicals and weapons that made widescale, unprecedented kill-offs increasingly likely.

This wasn't the Middle Ages when the plagues would strike without warning, killing up to a third of the population. Those mechanisms were poorly understood, often attributed to a God administering punishment for wrongdoing.

Modern plagues are radiation and toxic wastes — manmade, demystified, putting a bigger distance between us and the superstitious fear of God. As the relationship between "goodness" and reward slipped away, people began to doubt God's goodness, to question the entire moral framework, and to reject the old ways because they weren't working.

Our generation was born into this shadowy world.

Searching, Searching

Like millions of forties, I grew up in a world permeated by the Cold War and nuclear menace.

My father lived through two wars. He was too far from Europe to feel the full impact of the First World War, but he had the misfortune to be studying in England when the Second World War broke out, which meant he spent the next six years getting bombed, wondering what was going on at home, and trying to stay alive. He met my mother during that terrible war.

My father is an intelligent man with an open mind who favors the scientific method. He has a healthy mistrust of religious leaders who tell you how to live your life. He would prefer that you figure it out for yourself.

In part, he developed this mistrust reacting against his upbringing, which was dominated by a martyr-oriented branch of Islam still practiced in Iran today. Although raised a Muslim, my father eventually rejected the religion because it was too closely allied with a broad fatalism that froze the nation in its tracks. Whenever anything went wrong, people said, "It is the will of God," as if there was nothing they could do about it. My father left Iran forever when he was twenty-two years old.

In England, my mother was raised as a good Protestant. She didn't ask a lot of questions, preferring to accept that God was God and church was church, and that was the way it was. When she met my father and married, religion was not a big problem between them. Then my sister and I were born.

It is amazing how quickly parents who have ignored religion tend to think about it when they have children. Religion makes it easier to answer children's simple questions about what happens after people die and it helps to provide a moral framework that many parents have difficulty articulating independent of dogma. Curiously, my parents were an exception to this rule.

By the time I was seven or eight, my father suggested that I start attending all kinds of different church services, ranging from Baptist revival meetings to high mass, to Jewish ceremonies. He wanted me to see what was available, what made the most sense for me, before deciding on a religion.

For years, on Fridays, Saturdays, or Sundays, I would attend different services. I was terrified at Baptist Sunday school when a kindly old lady held out a piece of string and started tying knots to show what happens each time we tell a lie. Then, she held up a tiny ring representing heaven and showed how the string couldn't get through the ring to heaven if it had more than a few knots. That stunned me. If what she said was true, my knots would create a lump the size of my head! It was already too late to get to heaven and I was only seven. It looked like there was no hope with the Baptists for me.

At Catholic mass, I was awestruck by the ceremony, the smells of incense, and the echoes. But, once again, the religion seemed to stress punishment and denial rather than the love and compassion that they all said Christ symbolized.

I drifted through the solemn and joyful counterparts of Judaism, the fervor of Seventh-Day Adventists, and the quiet reasonableness of the

Quakers. I tried to reason with the Unitarians and argued with the Jehovah's Witnesses. I had tremendous difficulty understanding why the Anglicans and Catholics had two completely different churches when they were so similar. Everywhere I turned, a preacher or a priest told me that his religious sect was the only one, and all the others were wrong. It simply didn't make sense.

For a few years, I settled on the United Church as a simple compromise — not too extreme and not too self-righteous. It ended one day when the Sunday school teacher grabbed a stray dog that was starving and freezing and trying to find warmth in the church doorway and threw it down a flight of stairs. I took the dog home and left the church.

For twenty years, I considered myself an agnostic or an atheist. I really didn't want to believe in anything. Then, slowly, like a flower unfolding, my spirituality began to awaken. I wanted more answers, especially about death. I began looking for religion again.

This time, I explored the Eastern side, baffled by Hinduism but attracted to Buddhism for its peacefulness and focus on good works.

Although I haven't studied Eastern religions formally, I continue my reading and discussions as I search for a clearer picture.

Will the search get more frantic as I get older? Will I need the certainty of an afterlife or reincarnation to comfort me in my old age? Is fear of death the only real reason for having religion?

How Can I Be Sure?

A few hundred years ago, a bright French mathematician named Blaise Pascal summed up this religious question very neatly.

He said that belief in a God was a good wager or bet. If you were right, living a good life, you ended up in heaven.

If you were wrong and no God existed, you lived a good life anyway and weren't any the worse for it. Therefore, bet on the existence of God.

As gamblers, we seem to be hedging our bets a bit as we hit forty, leaning toward belief. If this is what it takes to make us kinder to other human beings, more decent and more caring, then the gamble is a good one.

There probably is an afterlife. I think there probably is. And I think that just to be safe, it pays off to
be a good guy, not to step on too many heads or
kill people, just in case. So I might as well play it
safe, be a good human being. You never know.
Ludwik, piano tuner

When I was younger, I felt really good when I was
going to church. Lately, it's just sort of coming
back. I was an altar boy and all that good stuff, but
I want to go back to church more. You know, you
want to cover your bases. I've done some things
I've regretted. I think we all have, and I don't know
if they're black marks or not.
Raoul, fisheries worker

We want to play it safe. What do we think we win with this wager?

Spirit in the Sky

More than half of the forties surveyed believe there is a real heaven and a
real hell. But almost half don't believe in heaven and hell at all.

Women are much more likely than men to believe in a real heaven
and hell. The smaller the city you live in, the more likely you are to
believe in a real heaven and hell. Conversely, the higher your income or
education, the less likely you are to believe. At forty, we are almost
equally divided between a literal concept of salvation and punishment
and an incredibly wide range of alternatives.

Those who don't accept the harps and pitchforks can't agree on the
alternatives. Some believe everything ends with death. Others are attracted to some form of reincarnation.

One side feels clear about the ideas of reward and punishment. The
other side doesn't buy cut-and-dried answers.

I feel like if you are good to people and you are fair
and you don't lie and you don't do bad things to

people, that if there is a heaven you will probably get there.
Winston, plating factory

I think there is a lot of misinterpretation about heaven and hell. It's the way that religious leaders hold power. You know, if you don't do this, you are going to fry.

But when you look at the numbers of people in books who have written about death and near-death experiences, have you ever heard of one where a guy says, "Oh yeah. All of a sudden I was in this valley full of fire and all these people were coming after me with pitchforks?" Never. Never.

I am far more tuned into the idea of reincarnation, past lives, that sort of thing. I have been a warrior in many lives. And I've hurt a lot of people. In Vietnam, my life was threatened. I had truly hellacious experiences of seeing men's faces being blown away in front of me and I think that was set up for me as part of my karma. This time round, I will be the peaceful warrior. Jesus said, "Heaven is here on earth." I think hell is here on earth too.
Ed, forest ranger

Forties are split down the middle. Half take a very traditional, hard-line Christian view. But even among this group, there is some latitude in defining precisely who goes to heaven and who goes to hell.

Will we go to hell if, as children, we tell a few little lies that are turned into a threatening knot on a string? Will we get to heaven if we steal, murder, or hurt others but then repent after a lifetime of cruelty five minutes before we die?

I was brought up in a pretty religious way with the Baptist idea of heaven and hell. Subconsciously, it colors my morality, although I think much more rationally about it now and have very little use for

> the kind of theology or people who talk about it.
> But it's still in me, and I think heaven and hell are
> something you create right here.
>
> So, heaven and hell in the conventional sense is
> something that I detest because I've seen so much
> damage done with it. But, in a general moral sense,
> I'm very aware of it, and every choice I make I
> think is based on whether it's going to be good for
> my spirit in the millennia to come.
> *Kerry, perfume manufacturer*

No matter how much we try to pull away from the religion we are raised with, it colors our thinking. We tend to stick with the tried and true.

Fewer than one in ten of us has changed religions in the last ten years. We feel more religious than we did ten years ago, especially blacks, among whom 58 percent said they felt "more religious." Yet, we attend religious services less frequently than we used to.

In part, it is because we are a "custom-designed" generation. We like the idea of picking and choosing to create religious structures with which we feel comfortable.

> I believe a little bit of a lot of different religions. I
> believe in reincarnation. I believe that I've had pre-
> vious lives. I don't attend any church in any regu-
> lar fashion, but I do pray.
>
> I thank God for all the wonderful things he has
> given me. And I think I am way more sincere at
> this particular point in time than I was when I was
> marched off to church six days a week as a kid.
> *Harriet, speech therapist*

We even experiment with religion. We have developed a clearer idea of ourselves and what we want. We know the recesses of the soul that need cleaning and those that will do just fine. So, we borrow from differ-ent spiritual sources, tailoring a set of beliefs that feels right for us.

If we are slightly more religious, experimental, and yet torn between firm belief and big questions, why do we get more involved in religion as we approach forty? One reason is for the children.

Show Me the Way

No matter how much we rebel against our upbringing, it sinks deep roots that put forth branches later in life. If we were exposed to religion as kids and we think we turned out okay, we are likely to turn back to religion for our own children.

Religion is especially attractive these days when issues of morality, ethics, and decency are autopsied on the nightly news with numbing sameness.

When the mayor does drugs and goes to hookers, when the army officer breaks the law and lies, when executives who poison whole towns are rewarded with fat bonuses, and it is all paraded for inspection every night on TV, it is very difficult to provide clear moral guidance for children. It's a time when many of us turn to religion.

> The driving factor is my son.
>
> Even though I have lost faith in the church, when I started thinking about it for my son I began remembering the silence and peace that religion gives you. So I have to make some moves. I think that he should believe there is a God because it's a good way to get him into the idea of ethics and what's right and what's wrong. Maybe there's a better way to do it, but I'm not that sophisticated.
>
> There's a whole school of thought which says you can develop ethics in a child and a sense of values without alluding to religion, but I think that religion does play a role in a mass culture and, why not give the religious upbringing and let him make the decision when he's older?
> *Peter, clothing manager*

I still believe there's a hell, and if I had children I

would raise them to go to church and understand
the importance of church, but I wouldn't tell them
or train them that if you didn't go to church you
were a bad person and would go to hell.
Kit, cocktail waitress

Comments such Peter's and Kit's upset the rigid fundamentalists of our day. The dogmatists want everything in black and white, with the brightest searchlight on the white and the darkest shadow on the black. However, millions of thinking forties find too many holes in the rigid world of light and shadow.

We want to have it both ways. We like the idea of heaven and hell with its ethical and moral certainty. However, we can't help cherry-picking and custom designing so that we can have it our way.

God

For many of us, religion consists of institutions and ceremonies. Sunday school, the church, baptism, communion, marriage, and funerals are just a few of the religiously oriented aspects of our lives. They permeate our consciousness and shape some of our behavior and decision making. As a result, we tend to talk about institutions and ceremonies much more than we talk about God.

After I had completed the interviews for this book, I noticed an interesting pattern. Hardly anyone spoke about God. Instead, we talked about church and other institutions that were supposed to be channels to God. It was almost as if religion could be "taken care of" by the institutions without talking much about spirit, God, or some other higher, animating force in the universe.

Perhaps we have become too complacent, assuming that institutions and specialists such as preachers and priests can do our spiritual work for us. Maybe we believe that by going through the motions we cover our bases with our particular version of God, and that is enough.

Yet, as we age, we can keep our spirit glowing only by looking for a closer, more direct connection with a higher being. If we don't, then our claims to be getting more religious may ring a bit hollow.

If you don't keep a direct connection to God every
day, something is lost. For me, it's like food, nour-
ishment. I need it on an ongoing basis or something inside me dies. I need to talk to God directly
through prayer, and if I go a few days without it, I
feel lost.
Lucinda, literary agent

Even though we say we are getting more religious, we don't talk
much about God. Perhaps our schooling and exposure to a wider world
through the media throw so many things at us that God isn't particularly
special but is merely part of a larger religious mix.

You Can't Fool All the People All the Time

We are the best-informed generation in history. Along with formal
schooling, we've seen more of the world on television in a week than
most of our great-grandparents saw in a lifetime.

From an early age, we have seen and experienced so much that we
question dogma or any "official" information about the way to do things.
If it doesn't ring true as measured against our experience, we become
suspicious. All information, especially from official sources, is given a
thorough evaluation.

When religious leaders gave us information, we tested it rather than
accepting it blindly. We tested it against what we saw, read, and experienced. Drawing on a wide range of sources, including books, films, television, and well-traveled friends, we were less likely to accept dogma
than was the generation before us.

Nowhere was this more evident than in the question of sex. Early
religious leaders realized that if they could make people feel bad or
uncomfortable about the basic human need of sex, they could get more
control over them. To this end, they twisted information, withheld facts,
and disseminated lies. In some cases, this did terrible psychological
damage. In others, it had hilarious results.

A visiting priest came in to see us when I was in

the eighth grade, and of course, at thirteen, I was an active little boy, kissing all the girls and doing all the things thirteen-year-old boys do.

And he stood at the front of the class and they separated the girls and put them in another room with a sister and they told the boys they were going to talk about sex. Now remember, this is our first contact with sex at the age of thirteen. And this wasn't back in the cave era. This was 1964 or something.

He said to our group of guys, "Your body is able to produce 2,000 ejaculations in a lifetime." And I grabbed my fuckin' heart and almost fell out of my chair. And I started counting on my fingers and toes and anything that was there, and to the best of my recollection, I figured I had reached 1,999.

I went home that afternoon and jacked off twice and figured that I got to 2,001 and that he was a liar, and I never trusted a Catholic priest after that. But I tell you, the beads of sweat were forming. When I hit 2,000, I was really hoping he wasn't right.

Peter, pharmacist

It's Too Late to Turn Back Now

Maybe we have a spiritual clock as well as a biological clock.

As you get older, religion gets into your thoughts a bit more.

Renja, motor vehicle license examiner

Like it or not, it is part of the human condition to try to make sense of death.

At forty, our spiritual clock is ticking a little louder. A friend may die suddenly. A parent passes away. Accidents happen. Diseases strike. We begin to wonder if there's more to life.

Therefore, we can be certain of one thing: We will focus on religion more in the years to come. If we weren't religious before, we will explore the subject. If we have drifted away from our church, we may reinvestigate its possibilities.

> I want to establish whether I could be convinced
> that there's some form of supreme being. I've
> always been a big believer in afterlife, mostly from
> the selfish impulse of not wanting to just be extin-
> guished. More and more, I've actually done a little
> Bible reading, a little bit of exploring of Christiani-
> ty and other things.
> *Ali, chef*

Increasingly, we are religious explorers. The New Age movement is an attempt to integrate mind, body, and spirit by exploring alternative ways of understanding all three. It includes stress on natural healing methods; a systematic exploration of the relationship between energy, health, and spirit; and the belief that everything in the universe is integrated even more completely than we understand. A small but influential group of pioneers is trying to figure out where the mind, spirit, and body meet. They are frustrated with many of the older religious structures that separate mind and body from soul, elevating the mind while dismissing the body as a disgusting shell for the soul.

These New Age pioneers will rewrite at least one chapter in the book on religion as they age.

But, for many, our exploration is in dribs and drabs, bits and pieces — a little Bible reading, a few thoughts about religion, or even toying with the idea of reincarnation.

> They say that there's a measurable amount of ener-
> gy in the room after a person dies. Even though I
> don't believe in heaven or hell, I toy with the idea
> of reincarnation. But I can't bear the thought that I

will be born as a child again. That I'd have to go
through this all again. I just couldn't bear it.
Bunny, dancer

As we explore religion, we explore spirituality. They are not the same
thing.

Religion is an organized structure for developing and focusing spirituality. Many people who say they are religious spend more time going
through the forms and prescriptions of religion than exploring the actual
spirit. Many who say they are spiritual feel that organized religions don't
give them the room to develop their spirituality fully enough.

I don't have a religion. But I've developed a spirituality.

When I started to learn about Eastern and East
Indian philosophy and reading things like Shirley
MacLaine's book, I laughed. When I first heard the
word *karma* in the 1960s, I laughed. I laughed at
the flower children. Until Vietnam.

That started me searching for something.

When I started reading about Eastern philoso-
phies and religions and karmic law and really
understanding them as an adult, it seemed so natural to me that it became easy to accept those prin-
ciples. Now I can understand why a lot of people
became Buddhist and embraced other doctrines
than the Western religions.

Toni, homemaker

At forty, spirit and religion rise up a little more in our consciousness.
This can be a positive, liberating experience — no matter what you finally decide is true.

For me, religion has been a struggle. I am attracted to karma — the
idea that a good life is repaid and a bad one relived. I am repelled by a
concept such as original sin because I think it is narrow-minded to
assume that we are born as shit and have to spend our lives climbing
out. I am open-minded enough to believe everyone has a right to his or

her own religious beliefs, but I draw the line when anyone tries to force those beliefs on me.

Unfortunately, because of people's statistical uncertainty about their own religious choice, they feel more comfortable making converts, whether through persuasion, warfare, or political manipulation. And I don't like coercive religion. It has nothing to do with spiritual growth.

Yet, it seems to be in our nature to want everyone to join the same religion as us. Recently, I had a remarkable conversation that showed me the type of gulf that can exist between religion and cultures.

I was dining with a self-made multimillionaire in his 20,000-square-foot home, with indoor swimming pool. Each year, he donated millions to his church and a group of very right-wing politicians. Between bites, he said, "Do you realize how terrible it is that, in China, the government doesn't let the people have religion? We have a duty to help them know about Christianity."

I was stunned. Didn't he know that most Chinese would return to their traditional religions, which include Confucianism and Buddhism, before they would turn to Christianity? When I mentioned this to him, he was honestly shocked. This rich, powerful man had not considered for even one moment the idea that more than a billion people might not choose his religion, given a choice. It troubled him throughout dinner and well into the next day.

After all, if a billion people disagreed with his choice, how could he be sure? And in his uncertainty, I find my own. What if I am wrong in all my experimentation? The only consolation I have is the fact that since only one religion can be right, most of the world will be joining me.

I have enough ego to be troubled by the idea that death is final. That the last breath does nothing but dissipate a tiny puff of energy into an expanding universe. After all, if we have worked so hard to make a good life, to work through our problems, surely that learning can be put to some benefit in the larger scale of things. And so, I am continually forced back to the essence of religion — the soul and spirit.

There are so many conflicting ideas of soul, including its origination, that I refer you to any good theological library for the details. For me, the soul is our essence, our center, our sense of being. It is where our energy originates and returns. It can either expand or contract.

If we are expanding, we are opening to the world around us, getting rid of anger, criticism, and cruelty. If we are contracting, we get smaller, holding everything closer, denser, and less alive.

We expand when we think it is safe to expand, when we see the world as part of us rather than apart from us. We expand when we can let go of fear, have faith, and assume that goodness is its own reward. That is the reason that faith is the basis of all major religions. We have to believe in something of which there is no firm proof. We must submit.

Nearly every major religion includes submission as the price of entry. My friend Nick says, "The price of admission is your submission." And ultimately, submission is the only way we can release ego, which is the force that blocks the soul. Submission is the core of all religious truth. Without submission to some higher power, our ego can run unchecked, our sense of self-importance can allow us to do terrible damage.

Already, the human race's collective ego has run unchecked for several hundred years. We have raped the earth, poisoned the waters, and torn a hole in the sky. We have done this because we've lost our relationship to spaceship earth. We assumed that human beings were the greatest good and that everything paled beside us. We have had unparalleled success in creating deserts, making species go extinct, and poisoning the air — all because we lost perspective.

Religion brings back perspective. We are an infinitesimal speck in the universe. There are a billion billion stars that we know about, and countless others we cannot measure. There are multiple billions of suns, potentially surrounded by planets filled with life-forms. There is so much energy in the universe that we don't know where it will ever end.

It is this energy that continues to attract me to religions that favor reincarnation. If Einstein was right and energy is neither created nor destroyed, then it has to go somewhere on our death. Yes, it could be a whisper of breath in a hurricane universe. Or energy could be reorganized into another life-form, which might even travel to another galaxy to work our karma.

Over the next forty or fifty years of my life, I am going to work on this. Will I end up a Buddhist? Possibly. Will I experiment and create my own tailor-made version of what happens after death? Probably.

To my mind, the simplest and most powerful key to unlock ourselves is "forgiveness." If we can forgive, we have made a quantum leap toward physical and spiritual health.

With forgiveness, we lose regrets. With forgiveness, we stop beating up on ourselves for being human and get on with the job of realizing our potential. To forgive, we have to let go of our ego, that part of us which wants to get even, to be the most important, to be the top dog.

We will draw on this capacity to forgive even more as we age. It will be more important to let go of attachments to the past, to set our sights on the best life we can make for ourselves.

During our journey through forty, we have stopped at jobs and money, reflecting on our need to provide for our old age. We have puzzled over the right plan for keeping healthy, wrestled with families, sighed over remembered loves, sung along with the Beatles, and tried to lay regrets to rest.

Let us shape these experiences, draw from them the essence of learning, and take a calculated guess at what life after forty will be like for us personally, and for our generation.

Life after 40: Where Do We Go from Here?

The Best Is Yet to Come

Forty has long been a symbolic crossroads. For our grandparents' generation, it was closer to the end of life. For us, it is smack in the middle.

At a crossroads, we have to choose which way to go, a decision that isn't always easy. As the famous baseball philosopher Casey Stengle reminds us, "If you don't know where you're going, you might get someplace else."

Too often, we find ourselves in places we don't want to be. A bad job. A wrong marriage. A frustrated life. Usually, we don't know how we arrived there.

On a moment's reflection, the reason is clear. We didn't know where we were going, so we got someplace else. This simple awareness holds the key for unlocking the full potential of life after forty.

Unless we create clear visions of what we want from our lives, there is a danger that we will drift without even noticing the current, until we turn around and ask ourselves why we are not getting closer to what we want.

The current moving our generation is very strong.

It is created by continuous technological improvement, which creates new communications, medicines, manufacturing processes, and service industries. The technological change simplifies some parts of our lives but introduces new difficulties, including how to deal with the stress, how to relate to our fellow human beings, and whether this is the world we want.

The current is accelerated by an exploding world population.

There is so much pressure on trees, water, and fossil fuels such as oil that we are asking, for the first time, about the limits of our planet. These changes have turned our ideas about status on their head. As we begin to look at the larger picture, we no longer attribute status to items that are contributing to the destruction of the world. Instead, we agree among ourselves that we can do without ivory, fur coats, bleached paper, gas-guzzling cars, and rare tropical hardwoods. Instead, we want the "elusive" quality of life.

At the center of the current, our Baby Boom, the best-educated, most highly experimental generation in history, is carried along. By our sheer size and shared ideas, we reshape the river that carries us. In our attempt to re-create our parents' world, we have pushed suburbs so far into the countryside that there is hardly any countryside left. We have pushed up housing prices, redefined the role of women, and empowered the media. In our quest for quality of life, we sought the holy grail of California and, in the process, redefined the West Coast. Many of us simply dropped out, creating communes in Oregon, New Mexico, and Massachusetts that still exist.

The current keeps moving. It is fast and strong. Yet, by observing it, knowing its characteristics, understanding people and technology, we can get a better handle on where we are going and what to do about it.

Where Are We Going?

Like most forty-year-olds, I am inherently optimistic about the future. It is an optimism born of confidence and awareness. At last, I have enough figured out to make things happen the way I want them. I have the confidence to actually try. I have come a long way since I was twenty.

At twenty, I really believed the world owed me a living, that, somehow, my sheer potential should be unlocked by others and I could just sit home and collect the check. At forty, I have a clearer picture of what to do, but I also know that I have to go out and do it. And that takes hard work. In this awareness, I am not alone.

> I think my forties are going to be a lot of hard work and a lot of slugging. And a lot of wheeling and dealing and finagling and maneuvering and swimming upstream. That was also how my twenties were. But the difference is, I know how to do it now. I am able to be responsible for my actions.
>
> I can change things now that I could not before, as I was subject to other people manipulating me and maneuvering me and telling me where to go and what to do and how to do it. Now I am in control of that. In that sense, my forties are going to be fabulous. But it is not going to be a piece of cake.
>
> I think the fifties will be the fruit of the labor. You know, of the accomplishment.
> *Jenny, bank manager*

We are optimistic and confident about our future. We know we will have to work to make it turn out right. But what do we have to look for in that uncharted terrain?

Money

The good news is that we are now entering our prime working years. During the next twenty years, we will make more money than we have ever made before. The difference between the next twenty years and the last twenty is that our focus will shift toward saving, paying down debt, and preparing for our "old" age rather than spending everything we make. This is going to confuse the so-called experts who expect our generation to move *en masse* into bigger houses, buy up fleets of luxury cars, take round-the-world cruises and spend, spend, spend.

To be sure, there will be some of us who make out really well. Money will be no object. But the vast majority will make out okay but won't be rich.

> I can see myself working for a long time. I am con-
> cerned about having enough income to support
> Billy's college and I want to be comfortable. I can't
> say whether I will be doing the same job I am
> doing now, but I can see myself busy.
> I like to keep myself busy, so I'll probably be
> working, and probably working around the house.
> Like, when we bought this house, I did all the
> plastering. I mean, this house was forty years old
> and had a lot of cracks, but I really enjoyed doing
> it. I see more of that. Keeping busy.
> *Beth, anthropologist*

The one wild card for all of us is inheritance. This "windfall" will be very irregular. Already, some lucky forty-year-olds have started to benefit from their parents' wealth. Richer families are transferring money now. This includes everything from loans to the down payment on a house, all the way through to trust funds for grandchildren.

But most parents cannot be too cavalier with their money. After all, they don't know how long they will live, what medical bills they might run up, or what they might need. So, the much-predicted massive inheritances for the Baby Boom will fall unevenly among the population, enriching some, embittering many.

No matter how noble we are at forty, there will be those of us who are frustrated by our parents' longevity, angry that they are holding onto money that we might use. Although this is a selfish, mean way of thinking, it is very real.

This concern over parents' inheritance prompted Joyce Carol Oates to write a short story about a cruise ship that took unwitting parents and dropped them on a desert island on their children's orders so that they could get at the inheritance more quickly. Fiction? As we get older, there will be more than a couple of sensational cases a year based on children who get rid of a parent because they can't stand waiting for the inheritance any longer.

On the flip side, more of us will be faced with the painful difficulty of taking care of an aging parent, most likely a mother. For some unfortunate families, it will stress finances, create personal strain, and force us to look deep into our hearts to discover where we stand on the issues of love, family, and responsibility.

But that is the negative side of the future. On the whole, the vast majority of parents and their children will work together to try to create the best possible financial scenario.

Lotta Lotto

Money, or the lack of it, can really confuse us. If we don't have enough, we can lose sight of what really matters and lose touch with our heart.

To find out what we are really like if money weren't an issue, I posed this question to forty-year-olds: "What would you do if you won $10 million tax free in a lottery today?" Ten million dollars in a lump sum after taxes is a lot of money. It lets us stretch our imagination beyond the immediate concerns. Our answers give us an idea of where our problems and hearts lie at forty.

If I Won $10 Million Tax Free Today: Top 5

	Men %	Women %
Spend	54	65
Invest/pay bills	44	55
Share with family and relatives	27	50
Give to charity and help others	25	31
Retire and do what I want	29	22

Oh, by the way, here are your chances of winning a lottery before your seventy-fifth birthday . . .

If you buy one lottery ticket a day, six days a week for thirty-five years, the chances of winning at least $1 million in a lump sum are about 1 in 1,000. This assumes a lottery such as Ohio's, where you must pick six numbers out of forty-four correctly.

If we suddenly came into money, the first thing we would do is spend on travel and family visits, on home and furniture, and on luxury and status items. In other words, true to Big Generation behavior, we would make our immediate life better.

Almost as soon as we finish spending, we would invest and pay bills. Women seem even more concerned than men with getting out of debt and putting money aside for the future.

When it comes to sharing with families, women are much more generous than men. Half of all forty-year-old women surveyed said they would share their windfall with relatives and family. Slightly more than a quarter of men did.

Women are also more generous than men when it comes to charity and helping others. On the whole, it was heartening to see that so many forty-year-olds would share their windfall with others less fortunate than them. It shows the generosity and good spirit that this generation will need as we age.

For me, the biggest surprise in forty-year-old behavior is the small number of us who said, "I would quit work if I won $10 million tax free today." I imagined that most of us would opt for the easy life. Instead, roughly a quarter would quit work. In other words, we feel that our jobs are important, that work itself has inherent value and we draw considerable strength from it. We like to keep busy, to feel that we are contributing. And this won't go away as we get older.

We are an active generation. We like to feel we are part of the action, whether as participants or observers. This promises to turn some of the myths of old age upside down. We will keep experimenting as we age.

It is very likely that many of us will enter politics for the first time at the age when our parents thought of retiring. There will be more late-starting artists than ever before, and even a few sixty-five-year-olds who challenge the courts and the universities by demanding admission to law school and medical school at what used to be called retirement age. Waving life-expectancy tables, we can point to the fact that even after we graduate we would have twenty years of practice ahead. We don't want to be bored.

> When I get older, I don't want to be bored, sitting
> around. I'm not going to be sitting around, smok-
> ing hashish with a bunch of morons. But I would

like to get involved with something totally different
from what I'm doing. For sure, I'm not going down
to Florida.

I would never move to Florida. I will go somewhere, probably with the Baby Boomers. It will be
a nice place. It will be comfortable and have medical facilities. I will be with people that I like, and
share values and ideas with them. My life's been
great. I assume this luck thing is going to continue.
And I don't know what's coming but I don't imagine myself living in some multimillion-dollar
home. Just comfortably.

Billy, computer service

Sixty Years On

Although we are optimists, trusting to our luck, eager to keep busy, we
could face serious problems thirty years from now. For those of us who
haven't saved enough money, government pensions may not do the job.
This will generate new levels of political activism, pitting a senior population against a younger, upcoming generation that doesn't want to pay
any more taxes. It will strain our ingenuity and imagination to solve this
dilemma.

This is especially important in light of the fact that approximately
750,000 Baby Boomers will live to be a hundred years old. Most will be
women.

It is hard to believe that so many of us will live so long. Among people who are forty years old *this year*, more than 35,000 will live to be
100. It freaks me out!

More than anything, it sends this clear message: If you are married
and a woman, make sure that your husband's pension and benefits are
transferable to you. Don't be afraid to discuss this now. Even though
most of us are uncomfortable talking about wills, estate planning, and
life after someone else's death, it is going to happen whether we like it or
not. By planning well in advance and making sure that we are covered
on as many bases as possible, we increase the likelihood that we will be

able to attend the party to celebrate the eightieth anniversary of Wood-stock.

But, long before we reach our hundredth birthday, we could run into some short-term medical problems that might upset our financial apple cart.

Doctor, Doctor

Yuck. I don't like doctors and I don't even like thinking about them. I don't like being sick, and I have a pathological aversion to hospitals. They remind me too much of my childhood. The smell alone is enough to turn me into a long-distance runner.

Yet, the experts tell us we will be seeing more doctors and more hospitals as we age. They point to the fact that we will all need reading glasses, many of us will need hearing aids, and we will be beset by all the aches and pains of aging.

The good news is that, unlike our parents' generation, most of us will keep our teeth. This might not sound like a big deal, but it is. Healthy teeth make it easier to eat healthy food, including all that fiber that is going to help us live a long time.

But, like it or not, more of us will get hit by arthritis, cancer, heart problems, and other nasty illnesses that wait patiently for us to grow older.

As an optimist, I am convinced that we can make a serious dent in the "inevitable" diseases of aging. But, the responsibility is on us. Our doctors can't keep us from getting sick. They can only try to make us well again. And the old saying that an ounce of prevention is worth a pound of cure has never been more important than at age forty.

We are a well-educated generation. Let's use it. There are hundreds of books, articles, and television programs that give us important tips about how to fight unhealthy aging. Over the next two decades, there will be at least one "important" new book every two years that will focus on how to stay healthy as we age. They will all draw loosely from three categories — nutrition, physical activity, and the power of the mind/spirit.

Let's face it, we're going to have bite the bullet sooner or later, so why don't we start now? It's time to get our eating habits and exercise patterns in line with healthy living.

Let's begin with the fact that most of our unhealthy eating is a result of habit, of what we are used to. Habit is such a strong force that it is the biggest reason we don't make positive changes in our life. Breaking a habit is very stressful if it is done quickly. We need to change slowly. But we want speed in our "scratch 'n' win" world. We want instant results.

Even though it has taken us forty years to gain more weight than we need, to develop bad exercise habits, and to learn to eat improperly, we somehow think we should be able to snap our fingers and change it all within twenty-four hours. When this doesn't work out, we become frustrated, say "I tried," give up, and revert to bad old habits. Since we are going to live another forty or fifty years, we can afford to take a little longer to develop healthy habits for the future. The best way to change a habit is to do it slowly.

Start out with just one meal a week that is low in fat, high in fiber, good tasting. Do that for a month. Then, the next month move to two meals a week. By the end of a year, over half your meals will be healthy, you'll like the taste, and you won't have even noticed the change in habit.

The same goes for exercise. Start out easy and slowly work toward a comfortable level. The easiest way to begin exercise is by walking. Walk briskly for ten minutes away from your house or apartment and then briskly back. That's twenty minutes! That's enough to get the cardiovascular system going, to give you a boost of energy, and to start you on the walking path. Of course, if you haven't done any exercise at all for years, you might want to check with your doctor before you start.

Last and probably most important is the need to develop a positive mental attitude. It's a cliché, but it works. I have proof in my own family.

My father is eighty-two years old and has terrible emphysema, a legacy of two packs of cigarettes a day for forty years. When he was first diagnosed, more than twenty-five years ago, the doctors all told him he would be in a wheelchair and on oxygen by his seventy-fifth birthday. On his seventy-fifty birthday, he traveled to Turkey with my mother, riding local buses over 700 miles into the interior, then walking, very slowly, to see many of the sights. He still has emphysema. In fact, doctors who examine him can't understand how he keeps going, why he is not a bedridden cripple. My father's answer is short and simple: "Keep active. Do what you can. Listen to your body." He is right.

Too often, we tell ourselves, over and over, that we are too tired, too sick, or too unhappy to take care of ourselves. By repeating the negative message over and over, we help these unpleasant prophecies come true. Of course, if we have been criticized and put down for forty years, it is very hard to find the faith and courage to look inside and love ourselves.

Usually, we have been criticized for so long that we don't recognize the destructive power such criticism has. We can't put our finger on exactly where we lost faith in ourselves. Insidiously, criticism could have taken many forms — a father who told us over and over that we would be a failure, a mother who said we had squinty eyes or weren't very pretty, parents who withheld love because we weren't perfect. Any or all of these criticisms could convince us that we are not lovable, that we are not worth anything. We internalize the negative messages when we are young and pull them out to reinforce self-destructive behavior as we age. How can we break out of this terrible trap?

Some of us find strength in the praise of others. We look to a husband, wife, or friend, and even to our children, to love us. We can draw on the love, feel better about ourselves, and get healthier.

For others, religion provides the answer. God's love lets us tap into the love inside ourself.

But too many of us say "I can't love myself" because "Sometimes I am mean" or "I like to hurt people" or "I'm worthless." I was hung up on that same hook until I read a remarkable little book called *The Lazy Man's Guide to Enlightenment* by Thaddeus Golas. This tiny book, written in a very 1960s style, gave me a great solution. It simply said, "Love yourself for being mean," "Love yourself for being imperfect," "Love yourself for making the same mistakes over and over." It is a liberating truth. Because self-love that is rooted in self-forgiveness is the most important step toward a positive mental attitude. It frees us from the negativity of others.

Once we open up in a positive way, refusing to attach to other people's unfair resentment or criticism (why do they criticize us anyway?), we are on the road to health.

Recent scientific studies have shown unequivocally that the mind has the power to lower blood pressure, reduce some tumors, and cure many forms of illness that defy conventional medical treatment. It all begins by loving yourself. Is that so hard to do? For many of us, it is.

It is difficult to have perspective on oneself. It is even more difficult to unravel destructive influences from our childhood all by ourselves.

Even though we are the best-informed generation in history, many of us still feel that therapy to help heal emotional wounds is for people who are weak. Nothing could be farther from the truth. It takes great strength to pull out the deep barbs that we have carried much of our lives. It takes courage to face our fears and get rid of them. Nearly all of us could benefit from some form of therapy. Otherwise, problems can fester and turn into even worse emotional and physical difficulties with the passage of time.

In spite of our best efforts with nutrition, exercise, and positive thinking, we will get sick from time to time. Many will have accidents and need medical care. On this front, the future will probably be better than the present.

Currently, American medicine is a curious mixture of brilliant, state-of-the-art technology and practitioners who aggressively protect their right to perform too much surgery and prescribe too many drugs. The cost of the system is out of control. On a per-capita basis, America spends more on medical care than any country in the world, yet ranks with some Third World countries in areas such as prenatal care. As we age, we will change this system.

Already, we Baby Boomers account for more than one-third of all voters in the country. Soon, we will run most businesses, hold most elected offices, and become the voice of the nation. Medical-care reform will be a priority as we watch our friends eaten up by impossible medical costs.

> I never thought about it much until my grandfather got sick with cancer and I couldn't believe how fast his $250,000 worth of medical coverage was gone. Then, they lost the house, their life savings, and he died anyway.
>
> It makes me sick. The doctor drove up in a Mercedes every day, looked at my grandfather for sixty seconds, and sent us a bill for $65 each time. I'm not alone. I am going to change this system.
> *Chip, lawyer*

It won't be easy to change the system, but we will. We will take care of ourselves. Part of the change will come from our own growing responsibility for our health. Another part will be the revamping of a system that stresses cure rather than prevention.

After all, three-quarters of a million of us will live to be a hundred. Some of us might want to stay healthy enough to try for sex on our hundredth birthday.

Golden Slumbers

There will be at least one hundred-year-old couple having sex around the middle of the next century. And I salute them in advance. But what about our sex lives between now and then? What can we look forward to?

On the whole, we will slow down a bit. But we will still have sex and enjoy it. Many of us who are divorced at forty will not remarry. Instead, we will date, have sex with new partners, and play out a slightly more mature version of the old dating game.

> I am serious about my relationships, but I don't
> have to be monogamous. If that's what works,
> that's fine. But, as I get older, I realize that fewer
> opportunities and fewer people may be available at
> different times and places.
>   I mean, they might be married or live in a dif-
> ferent city. You may find them fun to be with and
> engaging and exciting, but you can't be with them
> all the time. I mean, it's not like being a teenager
> where you have to go steady. However, if some-
> body came along that I wanted to go steady with,
> then . . .
> *Donna, fashion consultant*

As we age, there will inevitably be more problems with impotence. The good news is that we will talk about it more, read about it more, and work to solve the problem. Usually, impotence is a temporary problem, but some diseases can create it.

Sexually explicit videos and magazines will experience increased sales to a senior population as boredom and declining energy set in. We will start to eliminate the stereotype of the "dirty old man" and substitute the idea that men will look at pictures of naked women, regardless of their age. And women will look at men. There's nothing inherently better or worse about a voyeuristic eighteen- or fifty-eight-year-old. That statement is bound to get a few moralists up in arms, but it is a fact of life. Sex will be fun, a little slower, and a little less frequent. We will talk about it a lot, probably sounding like latter-day "Golden Girls."

All You Need Is Love

What will happen to the family as we get older? And what will it mean to us?

Each year between 1993 and 1998, more than 4 million Americans will turn forty. And each year, just under 1 million will still have no children. In other words, we are not reproducing fast enough to keep the population growing. In fact, without immigration, it will probably go down. What does all this mean?

It means that our parents are lucky. They have, on average, between two and four children who will try to take care of them. Although the burden will fall disproportionately on women, especially unmarried women, we will all work hard to take care of our parents. There will be family fights, arguments, and even bitter divisions over this responsibility, but we will muddle through. But who will take care of us when we are old?

We forties don't have a lot of children. Barely 17 percent of forty-year-olds surveyed have three children. Most of us have one or two. And the way we all move around the country, there is no guarantee that our children will be close enough to drop over for a visit, take us to the doctor, or have us move in with them.

We will have to be resourceful as we age. A small but influential number of us have already experienced communal living, sharing and helping one another out. I am convinced that we will draw on these dormant skills as we get older. Just as we have experimented with trial marriages, dropping out of college, changing jobs, and putting off childbearing, we will create new living patterns in the twenty-first century.

This will be especially important for the millions of Boomers who have no children. There will be no one to care for us, but we are likely to have more savings and pensions because we have not had to bear the expense of childrearing. This leaves us with an even more interesting problem. When today's forty-year-olds who have no children die, who will we leave our money to? We are likely to endow foundations and other systems to help those less fortunate than us.

We have sufficient time to take responsibility for our lives. And strong marriages and relationships will make it easier. The good news is that our marriages and relationships are likely to get much better as we age — not only because we read about how sensitive we should be in every magazine, but also because of fundamental changes in us.

> I have heard that men get less ambitious and less career-oriented as they age and become more concerned with relationships. Women, on the other hand, tend to be more career-oriented because their kids are older and they are not tied down.
> So maybe men will do some thinking about where they have been. And maybe this is going to be nicer for us women because we'll actually be able to talk about feelings instead of the mortgage.
> *Petra, homemaker*

I see a very healthy future for the family. Not the old-fashioned family where the father's word was law, even if he didn't know what he was talking about. Not the old-fashioned family where children were protected from the world by a mother who was supposed to be protected from the world. Rather, families based on choice and love. At last, we are accepting that children have rights, that they are human beings with their own personalities. By treating children as fully realized human beings who need guidance and structure, we set the foundation for healthier families in the future.

The one dark spot is the urban ghetto where families are torn to pieces by poverty, violence, and despair. We have a moral and social responsibility to help solve those problems. And it all begins with the children.

If we can help make sure that children are properly fed, properly housed, and free from brutal intimidation, we give our society a leg up on the future. My biggest worry about the future of the family is that too many of us Boomers will put our children in private schools and turn our backs on the universal education that made Western nations great. I find it hard to believe that so many educated, affluent Baby Boomers are putting children in private schools and turning their back on the importance of quality education for all. Without education, there will be no one to do the highly sophisticated technical jobs of the future. Yet, the very people who have the money and influence to help are often saying that it is somebody else's problem. If we act like Victorian Englishmen and pretend that poverty and inhumane living conditions are some sort of necessary force in God's universe, we do ourselves and future generations a terrible disservice.

As we age, we will continue to experiment, especially with living conditions. It is very likely that we will form old-age "communes" where we share responsibility and compassion for one another. There will be two big differences between these communes and nursing homes.

First, we won't put ourselves totally in the hands of outsiders who will make every decision for us, including what we will eat and where we will sit. That form of paternalistic dominance was acceptable for our parents' generation. It won't be for us.

The second difference will be the fact that we will try to help and take care of one another. The power of the commune will spring from those generative intangibles love and compassion. We will all be in the same boat, pulling our oars to move in the same direction.

From this will come enormous strength, purpose, and a desire to continue living.

Paul McCartney's Sixty-fourth Birthday

Our future will be overcommunicated. We will have too many options and too many choices when it comes to entertainment and information.

We will try to deal with this by using two techniques: reverting to the past and looking for more specialization.

There's no question that we will be singing Beatles' songs at retirement age. Just as our parents get misty-eyed singing early Frank Sinatra songs, we will do the same with Elvis, the Beatles, and the Stones. And our kids will laugh at us, thinking that we are old fogies. And we will listen to their music and say that music just isn't as good as it was when we were young.

We will experience incredible nostalgia for the 1960s, praising its best characteristics and ignoring its worst. We will remember the idealism, shared purpose, and faith of the 1960s. Most likely, it will be part of our overall nostalgia for youth.

On the technological side, our futures will be safer and cleaner. Already, we are making aggressive inroads against pollution. As we demand better quality of life, this will lead to cleaner air and water and safer food. Unfortunately, it will take a long time to repair the damage we have done. But it will happen.

As we age, we will benefit from the computer revolution, which still rolls on unchecked. Everything from home security to medical diagnosis will be made easier by the computer. By the time we retire, most homes should have smart phones with computer capability that will make shopping, communication, and security easier.

Although the full benefits of the computer revolution will be realized by our children, we will still gain enormously. To be sure, our reflexes will be a little slower, which means that Nintendo will have to put out "senior" versions of their games. But, what the heck. We are up for the challenge.

The Spirit Is Willing

The most far-reaching change in our future will be in the area of religion. We will talk about it more, explore it more, and challenge it more. As we get closer to the final curtain, we will become more uncomfortable with the knowledge that most of us are going to make the wrong choice for an afterlife since only one version can be right.

This will test the limits of our tolerance in the years to come. If we are frightened by people who hold different religious beliefs, believing that their salvation threatens ours, we will begin to demand greater support for our own religion. This suggests that a small but very vocal group of aging Baby Boomers will literally try to shout down other religions.

On the flip side, millions of us will continue experimenting, trying to custom-design a religion that feels just right for us. The majority of these experiments will take place around Christianity, our de facto state religion. However, many experiments will involve reincarnation, because we are reluctant to leave life on earth.

To a large extent, we have been a coddled generation. Most of us have never gone hungry for more than a day, never lived in a house with no heat or indoor plumbing, and never believed the economy could completely collapse. Things have been pretty good for us. Materially, we have made out okay. We have more toys and entertainment than our parents could have dreamed of. Television itself is a miracle. We enjoy our comforts.

In sharp contrast, major religions were predicated on an awful life that was hard, unpredictable, and short. Life on earth appeared as a pale alternative to an eternal paradise after death. Our lives have not been that bad.

For that reason, we want to continue to enjoy life. For many of us, it is attractive to think that we would remain on earth after death rather than heading out into a heaven that may be spiritually uplifting but doesn't sound like fun. And we sure like to have fun.

Since we want to stay on earth and get more time here, reincarnation has a special charm. I am convinced that, as our generation ages, a large minority will seriously explore the possibility of reincarnation.

The New Age movement will continue to gain momentum as we look for religion that is holistic. The integration of spirit into a more "natural" order will gain adherents with each passing year.

Time, Time, Time

Each year after forty, it will feel as if time were speeding up. The more pressured we feel by time, the more we will feel that we have to make choices now that we have been putting off for years. The especially important choices include decisions about whether we want to stay in the job we have, whether we want to stay in the marriage or relationship we have, and how much we really care about ourselves.

> There is not enough time. I just can't understand where it goes. It wasn't April last month and here we are in July. It just goes by so quickly. That is the thing that scares you a little bit, saying "Jesus, what's going on?" It is not just the chronological thing of turning forty.
>
> Instead, you want it to stop. It's like everything was in slow motion before and then, in the thirties, it hit you in regular motion and now it feels like every-thing's going high speed. And I want to slow it down because I am in the prime of my life. I feel that.
> *Jake, golf pro*

Sometimes, I am totally freaked out by how fast time is moving. I think back on an event and say, "That was about three years ago" and my wife hauls out the calendar and says, "No, it was seven years ago." What happened to four years?

There is only one way to get a handle on time. That is to focus more completely on the present, the here and now. It is the old cliché of "stop-ping to smell the flowers."

As a generation, we have been inherently future oriented. Even as we partied during high school, we looked ahead to college. While we par-tied in college, we looked ahead to our jobs and the lives that society would carve out for us. Once we got those jobs, we began looking ahead toward promotions, pension plans, a bigger house, and everything else that money and responsibility bring. Somewhere along the way, we lost sight of the moment.

If you put this book down right now and just stop everything you are doing for a moment, you will be amazed at how long that moment is. Quietly, concentrate on your breath going in and going out, maybe two or three times. That is "the moment," the "now." It was only a few sec-onds, but it felt like a long time.

If we are going to be free of time panic, we should pull back from future focus, pull away from nostalgia, and try to engage in the immediate moment.

Often, the first thing that happens when we focus in the immediate moment is the realization that we don't like a lot of things that are going on right in it. That is why we tend to focus on the future or the past, to get away from what we don't like. But, take a moment to look at what you don't like, and instead of being bummed out about it, think about how it can be changed.

During the next ten years, this time implosion, where we are crushed by an understanding of time's weight, will force millions of us to finally get the courage to make positive changes in our lives. Those who make the changes will go through short-term stress in exchange for long-term health and happiness. Other millions will chicken out, giving in to what other people expect of them and saying, "We are too old for change."

As the clock ticks louder, we get a sense that we have to hurry up and have what we really want because we won't get another chance. Under time's relentless pressure, sometimes we focus on running away. We decide what we don't want and run away from it. Often, this means divorce, a change in jobs, or a move from one place to another. All too often, when we have made the change, we don't feel any better because we have run away from something we didn't want rather than toward something we did want. As Casey Stengle said, "Know where you're going."

One of the best things you can do for yourself at forty is to take out a piece of paper and write down your perfect life as you imagine it. Don't show it to anybody when you write it down. Just do it for yourself. And describe it in as much detail as possible. Take a look at what you really want once you've covered a page or two with details. Patterns will emerge.

Don't block your thinking by saying, "But I can't have that job" or "But my wife (or husband) won't approve of that." Think about what you want — not what someone else wants.

Put the description away for a few days and then take it out again and go over it. What seems to be most important to you? That is what you want. If you focus on having it, you are more likely to be happy, healthy, and fulfilled as you age.

The Vision

I have a really clear idea of what I want from my own life. And I developed it only a few years ago. Before that I was adrift. Now, as a Baby Boomer at forty, I think I might be able to achieve it.

At age thirty, I never knew what it meant to create the life I wanted. I didn't even know what life I wanted. I didn't even know I had a choice in the matter. Somewhere inside of me, my parents' Depression era, Second World War fear kept colliding with my sixties optimism and hope. Banging into each other, fear and hope create a lot of confused energy, which get in the way of clear vision.

Throughout my thirties, I was confused. I married a self-destructive woman who couldn't help herself out of a downward spiral. I endured a job that created a lot of stress and didn't fully satisfy me. At times, the money was okay, but I still felt lost.

Toward the end of my thirties, I finally acknowledged that I was terribly unhappy with my life, but I didn't know what to do about it. I still couldn't imagine that I could have the life I wanted. After all, my parents hadn't had it. Most of their friends hadn't had it. Why in the world did I have a right? Was it simply sixties optimism run amok? Was I kidding myself? More important, why was I afraid to articulate what I really wanted? Because I was afraid that if I dreamed and was disappointed, it would crush me. What a stupid way to live! That is when I decided I had to make a change.

I did something that many of us will do around our fortieth birthday: I made up a list of exactly what I wanted in my life, right down to the type of house and place in which I wanted to live. Then I listed the aspects of life as I was currently living it, my current reality. From that moment on, I took two essential steps.

First, I told everyone what I hoped to do and asked for help in achieving my goals. I knew that I would have to appreciate time delays, the inevitable extra months or even years it takes to make a significant midlife change. Second, I began to create a plan to move me from my current reality toward my dream.

When I made my list of what was really important in life, a few things jumped out from the page: a beautiful, clean, warm environment; my wife, Pat; time to live in and contemplate the moment; and sufficient income to enjoy it. My focus went to Hawaii.

I want to live in Hawaii because I love the climate, the landscape, and the clean air. Like millions in my generation, I want to go back to the country and have a garden that gives me year-round fresh vegetables and produce. I want a home where I never have to turn on the heat or the air-conditioning, choosing to open or close windows instead to keep the temperature the way I want it. As a northerner who has suffered through interminable winters with central heating that dries the skin and sets up electric sparks everywhere, I want the world's biggest humidifier, the Pacific Ocean, around me.

Along with the physical side of it, I want the intellectual side. My solution is to open the Pacific Think Tank on Maui. It will have two different purposes.

The first purpose will be to provide me with an income. By sitting in the middle of the Pacific Ocean, between the west coast of America and the Pacific Rim, my company will be uniquely situated to provide global advice on business in a rapidly changing world. Specializing in changes brought about by the aging Baby Boom, I will be able to provide state-of-the-art information to clients from different cultures. In an age of satellites, faxes, and fiber optics, I realize that it is possible to live anywhere and still be in touch with the whole world.

The second purpose will involve the free exchange of ideas between Hawaiian residents and the rest of the world. Each Thursday morning, I will invite anyone who feels like attending to a three-hour, free-coffee-and-donuts, free-for-all discussion about ecology, media, marketing, personal growth, Hawaii, and more. I am convinced it will attract its share of jet-lagged executives who have been awake since 5:30 in the morning, are bored with playing golf, and wouldn't object to stretching their minds a bit. At the same time, it should attract bright local residents who want to expand their world-view while contributing their unique personal knowledge. The Thursday-morning sessions will be free for anyone who wants to come.

That is my dream. Some might say it is aiming too high. Maybe it is. But, currently, I am working on how to make it a reality.

I know that my dream is different from those of my generation. Most Baby Boomers who have clear goals at forty focus their dreams on such satisfying visions as providing a good education for their children; getting out of debt; having a nice house; retiring with a good pension; possibly having a vacation home. These are beautiful dreams to work toward.

But, if you are one of the millions who are unsure, take time to work on the vision, the visualization. It will pay enormous dividends.

> There's one area I'm very weak in and I'm working on that now — visualization. It's a watchword of our generation. And I know my life is in my control — that's one thing I'm very sure of. I'm a little uncertain about how I'm going to fulfill my financial goals, so I'm still struggling with the idea of a dual profession, something that is dependable but will allow me some freedom of choice. That's not a solid image of the future, and I know that. So I'm working on creating a solid picture that I can create for myself.
>
> I do feel that to have a comfortable life is a very strong goal. To enjoy good beer, not the cheap swill, to be accepted by my peers and my career and to do it in such a way that I can have a comfortable life.
>
> *Darryl, singer*

Feeling Better

For some reason, a lot of Baby Boom futurists paint a scenario of our generation eating cat food from tins and living in abject poverty and misery. They focus on the worst aspects of physical existence without giving a moment's consideration to the inner peace and happiness that personal growth can bring. Religious history in every culture is loaded with people who shine from within, who have found self-love, forgiveness, and compassion, even though they don't have a lot of money. Millions of us will find that light within ourselves.

We won't become saints or mystics. Rather, we will get more comfortable with ourselves. We will forgive ourselves more easily and drop the worst of the emotional baggage we have carried for the past twenty to thirty years. We think it is going to keep getting better.

> People will really genuinely like me and think of me as a sincere, giving, caring, very bright human being. I'll be far more forgiving of everyone, including myself, as I get older. I'll be far more tolerant.
>
> I'll learn to enjoy myself, relax and have more fun. I'll have the best sex I've ever had in my life right into my nineties and hundreds. I will write and sing and paint and just be. And I think it will be the best time of my life.
>
> *Irene, human resource manager*

Not everyone aspires to Utopia over the next forty years. Most of us look for simple comfort and balance in our lives.

> I would like to be — this is just a very vague image — teaching someplace and writing, and I would like to have a kind of a getaway, you know, a second home. Maybe do some traveling and get involved in some kind of cause outside myself. Some kind of community-good type thing.
>
> I am looking forward to more time to myself. And more solitude so that I can think. And I am looking forward to enjoying my career and not having to work so hard. There was a time when I was working three jobs and getting my Ph.D. and raising my three girls by myself, and that was hell. Talk about hell. And I am not going to do that anymore. It is more balanced. I am looking forward to that continuing.
>
> *Joanne, biochemist*

Further Confessions of a Forty-Year-Old

I still have mixed feelings about forty. But, on the whole, I think it is a fabulous age. We are old enough to know what we're doing and young enough to do it. I feel good about the future.

When I started out researching my generation, the experts told me that Baby Boomers are more different from one another than they are similar, that the popular image of Baby Boomers who were hippies and then yuppies is a myth. Most good books about the Baby Boom focus on those differences.

But, at forty, I find we share more similarities than differences. We are concerned about our future and nostalgic for our past. We have an opportunity to affect positively the next half of our life. Midlife is bringing us closer together.

We are forced to look at the same agenda. It includes money and job, health, religion, and family. Inherently, we are looking back to the same past, weighing it, reanalyzing it, and even having fun with it. This brings up regrets, the Beatles, and so many landmarks.

We share a heritage. Whether we agree with one another about psychedelic drugs, we know they had an impact on our generation. Whether we liked the Beatles or the Stones, most of us agree about the importance of rock 'n' roll. And whether we are happily married or still single, we find a common ground for discussion in the sexual revolution. These items bind us more closely than we may have imagined.

As I researched this book, I kept realizing how much I have in common with forty-year-olds of my generation. I don't have a pension that's worth much. I am concerned about my family aging. I need to get in shape. Writing this book has started me moving in the right direction.

I am determined to start putting some money, any money, into a savings plan toward the time when I am older. I am going to gradually introduce more exercise and better eating habits into my life. I think I will start with a simple ten-minute walk away from my house and then back each day.

I am letting go of regrets. They don't help me anymore, and they force me to focus on the past.

When it comes to my family, things are still a little fuzzy. I am concerned about my parents as they age, and it worries me some nights when I can't shake it from my mind.

In my marriage, things are getting better. I have found a workable balance between my personal needs and the compromises that marriage forces upon us. My wife, Pat, is doing fine with the same struggle.

Spiritually, I continue to grow. Although it is difficult, I work on forgiveness and love. I have shed some of my natural attack mechanisms, but, from time to time, I can't help putting in a zinger against someone or something, especially the pompous or hypocritical. I am certainly not headed for sainthood.

I feel good about forty. It seems most of us do.

The next forty or fifty years will be fascinating, challenging, maddening, and ultimately liberating. I look forward to experiencing them with you.

For the Number Nuts

If you didn't get your fill of numbers and statistics in the body of the book, this section highlights some of the more interesting or startling findings of the survey.

Whenever you read a table of numbers, read it down, not across. Also, some columns add up to more than 100 percent, because people were allowed to make more than one choice or because of rounding.

Chapter 2: Landmarks

The Death of Martin Luther King

To most forties, Martin Luther King's death was not as important as John Kennedy's. The exception was among blacks, for whom King's death was as important as Kennedy's.

Interestingly, Martin Luther King's death was very negative to all forties except blacks, many of whom saw his death as an unfortunate but necessary martyrdom on the road to civil rights.

Importance of Martin Luther King's Death

	Male	Female	White	Black
	%	%	%	%
Extremely important	14	15	7	80
↓	15	13	14	10
	28	27	30	9
	18	24	23	—
Not at all important	24	20	24	—
Don't know/No answer	1	2	1	1

205

	Male	Female	White	Black
Was it positive/negative to you?				
Positive	16	14	12	41
Negative	75	77	79	50
Don't know/No answer	10	9	9	9

The Death of John Lennon

The death of John Lennon symbolized the end of an era. There would be no Beatles reunion. There would be no chance for the aging Baby Boom to collectively re-experience the magic of their youth.

John Lennon's murder capped a decade of inflation, terrorism, and unprecedented socioeconomic change. Therefore, it's not surprising that nearly 80 percent of all forties surveyed viewed it as a negative experience. Nonetheless, the vast majority of respondents said that although his death was negative, it was not important to them. Close to 50 percent said it was not at all important. It was slightly more important to forties with a postgraduate education; on the whole, the importance of his death increased in direct proportion to level of education.

Importance of John Lennon's Death

	Male	Female
	%	%
Extremely important	5	3
	6	8
	20	18
	19	24
Not at all important	48	56
Don't know/No answer	1	1
Was it positive/negative to you?		
Positive	6	6
Negative	80	79
Don't know/No answer	14	14

Vietnam

To most forties, Vietnam was important and negative. However, there was an important exception to this overall result: More than one in five forties were positive about Vietnam. This response was strongest among those who lived in small towns (population less than 50, 000), earned less than $30, 000 a year, and had only grade school education.

Importance of Vietnam

How important?	Sex			Population of City		
	Male	Female	Less than 50,000	50,000–499,000	500,000–1.99 million	2 million plus
	%	%	%	%	%	%
Extremely	50	40	43	44	39	50
↓	26	25	26	28	26	24
	16	23	21	20	24	17
	2	5	4	1	6	4
Not at all	4	5	4	5	4	5
Don't know/ No Answer	1	2	2	1	1	1

	Income			Education			
	Less than $30,000	$30,000–$49,000	$50,000 plus	Grade School	High School	College	Post-graduate
	%	%	%	%	%	%	%
Extremely	46	49	39	45	44	43	51
↓	21	26	32	18	23	29	26
	20	17	23	24	21	19	18
	4	4	3	–	5	3	2
Not at all	7	4	2	11	6	4	1
Don't know/ No answer	2	1	1	2	2	1	2

Was it positive/ negative to you?	Sex			Population of City		
	Male	Female	Less than 50,000	50,000–499,000	500,000–1.99 million	2 million plus
	%	%	%	%	%	%
Positive	25	21	31	21	18	20
Negative	68	73	62	72	74	74
Don't know/ No answer	7	6	7	7	9	6

	Income			Education			
	Less than $50,000	$30,000–$49,000	$50,000 plus	Grade School	High School	College	Post-graduate
	%	%	%	%	%	%	%
Positive	31	21	14	42	31	18	8
Negative	60	74	79	47	62	77	85
Don't know/ No answer	9	4	7	11	8	6	7

Virginity

Technology changed our sex lives.

We reached puberty as part of a disproportionately large generation. Within a few years, a new technology, the birth control pill, came on the scene, removing in one instant the greatest fear connected with premarital sex—unwanted pregnancy.

In the light of this, how do forties feel about losing their virginity?

On the importance scale, it ranked around the middle, about half way between extremely important and not at all important. It was more important for women than for men.

On the whole, it was a positive experience, but more so for men than for women.

Indeed, 25 percent of all women said it was a negative experience.

Importance of the Loss of Virginity

	Male	Female
	%	%
Extremely important	20	32
	14	21
	28	25
	12	5
Not at all important	21	13
Don't know/No answer	5	3

Was it positive/negative to you?

Positive	73	62
Negative	13	25
Don't know/No answer	14	13

The Pill

Attitudes toward the birth control pill were not much different from those toward the loss of virginity.

On the whole, the pill was a positive experience that was more important to women than to men.

Importance of the Birth Control Pill

	Male	Female
	%	%
Extremely important	16	39
	19	17
	27	17
	11	8
Not at all important	26	19
Don't know/No answer	1	1

Was it positive/negative to you?	Male %	Female %
Positive	66	72
Negative	22	21
Don't know/No answer	11	7

Chapter 3: Money and Work

Changing Bosses

If we believe TV and the movies, we forties change jobs as often as we change our underwear. This view was particularly prevalent during the "go–go" eighties, when it seemed as if everyone was changing jobs for a $2 raise and a cup of coffee.

In fact, nearly half (44 percent) of forties have had the same employer for at least ten years.

One in five has changed jobs only once. This suggests that, by the time we turn thirty, we have a fairly clear picture of what we want to do with our jobs and careers, at least for the next decade.

Changing Employers

Number of times changed employers in the past ten years	Male %	Female %
None	46	42
Once	23	20
Twice	12	13
Three times	7	12
Four times	5	4
Five or more times	6	4
Don't know/No answer	0	6

Reasons for Changing Employers

If you changed jobs during the past ten years, you most most likely did it for more money and better benefits or for greater opportunity for advancement.

If you're a woman, you are twice as likely as a man to have changed jobs to avoid stress.

Also, women are more likely than men to change jobs because they've moved. Although the numbers are lower than they were in the past, women still relocate almost three times as often as men.

Education played a big role in decisions to change jobs. The less education you have, the more likely you are to change jobs for money and benefits. The more education you have, the more likely you are to change jobs, in search of greater opportunity.

A note to employers: Be especially careful to give your postgraduate employees opportunity and interesting work, or they will leave. One in five forties with a postgraduate degree changed jobs during the last ten years, looking for more opportunity. One in ten changed jobs, looking for more interesting work.

Major Reasons for Changing Employers
(by Level of Education)

	Grade School %	High School %	College %	Post-graduate %
More money/Better benefits	29	16	14	10
More opportunity	5	7	13	21
Less stressful	–	6	6	4
More interesting	3	4	4	10

Do You Like Your Job?

Most of us like our jobs. Almost one-quarter of us love our jobs.

Not surprisingly, the more money we make, the more we like our job. This suggests that, by age forty, we have experimented sufficiently in the work force to find jobs that make us happy.

Feelings about Primary Job

	Male %	Female %
Love it	22	27
Like it	52	45
Neutral	14	10
Dislike it	7	4
Hate it	1	2
Don't work	4	10
Don't know/No answer	1	4

How Am I Doing Relative to My Expectations?

If someone had asked you ten years ago how you would be doing at age forty, you would have said "I'll be better off."

Nearly 62 percent of forties thought they would be better or much better off today than they were ten years ago. But they aren't.

For blacks, the number skyrockets. More than three out of four blacks thought they would be better off today than they are.

Ten Years Ago, Did You Think You Would
Be Better/Worse Off at Forty Than You Are Now?

	Male	Female	White	Black
Much better off	17	14	14	25
Better off	47	46	46	53
About the same	28	29	30	19
Worse off	8	9	9	1
Much worse off	1	0	1	1
Don't know/No answer	–	1	1	2

But, it's important to keep expectations in perspective. Close to 70 percent of forties feel they are better off than their own parents were at age forty. In other words, we've done better than our parents when they were forty, but we had such high expectations that we thought we could outdistance them by enormous margins.

Better or Worse Off Than Parents and Peers?

Ten years ago, we thought we would be better off than our parents. That was at age thirty. By age forty, we are less likely to compare ourselves with our parents and more likely to compare with others our own age.

Are You Better/Worse Off Than Your Parents When They Were Forty?

	Male	Female
	%	%
Much better off	28	30
Better off	42	36
About the same	18	19
Worse off	10	12
Much worse off	2	2
Don't know/No answer	2	2

Gazing into our crystal ball, how do we think we will compare with our peers in ten years' time, when we are fifty?

On the whole, we are optimistic realists. More than half of us think we will be better off. Men are more optimistic and more competitive than women. More than 57 percent say they will be better off than their peers ten years from now.

Will You Be Better/Worse Off Than Your Peers Ten Years from Now?

	Male	Female
	%	%
Much better off	11	11
Better off	46	39
About the same	36	41
Worse off	5	6
Much worse off	1	1
Don't know/No answer	1	2

Retirement and Pension

When it comes to retirement and pensions, the news is not good. Nearly half of all respondents rated their own retirement/pension savings plans as adequate at best.

Most shocking is the fact that 13 percent of men and 18 percent of women have no retirement/pension plan at all at age forty. This worrisome statistic is even more troubling when we note that 14 percent of college graduates have no retirement/savings plan.

On the whole, the only groups who rated their pension plan as more than adequate were those making more than $50,000 a year or those with postgraduate education.

With twenty-five years to the theoretical retirement age, we forties are going to have to play a lot of catch–up.

Rating Your Retirement/Pension Saving Plan

| | Sex | | Income | | | Education | | | |
	Male	Female	Under $30,000	$30,000–$49,000	$50,000 plus	Grade School	High School	College	Post-graduate
	%	%	%	%	%	%	%	%	%
Very good	14	11	6	14	17	5	10	14	15
Good	23	23	16	26	28	13	21	23	31
Adequate	30	27	27	31	28	37	29	29	26
Poor	15	16	18	14	14	8	16	15	17
Very poor	5	4	5	5	4	5	5	4	6
Have none	13	18	28	10	8	32	20	14	5

Chapter 4: Health and Staying Alive

Fitness

The road to health is paved with good intentions. Because, if nothing else, at forty, we have good intentions.

Most of us have not done much to improve our physical fitness within the past year. More than 50 percent of us did only a little or nothing. In spite of all the warnings, admonitions, and pleas by government, doctors, and health club operators, we just haven't quite stirred from our cars or our favorite TV–watching chairs to do something about it.

Fewer than 20 percent of us say we have done a lot to improve our physical fitness. Among this group, there is a direct relationship between education and improving fitness: The more education, the more improvement.

But, since the road to health is paved with good intentions, a much greater percentage of us intend to do something next year to improve our well-being. Once again, the more education you have, the more likely you are to plan on making a big change next year.

Did You Do Something to Improve Your Physical Fitness Last Year?

| | Sex | | Education | | | |
	Male	Female	Grade School	High School	College	Post-graduate
	%	%	%	%	%	%
A lot	18	20	11	16	21	26
About the same	33	27	42	27	29	35
A little	31	30	18	34	32	22
Nothing	19	21	29	22	17	18

Will You Do Something Next Year to Improve Your Physical Fitness?

	Sex		Grade School	High School	College	Post-graduate
	Male	Female				
	%	%	%	%	%	%
A lot	28	33	29	25	33	37
About the same	41	34	29	37	38	40
A little	23	27	26	27	24	20
Nothing	8	6	16	10	4	2

Thirty Versus Forty

Are we doing as much exercise today as we did at thirty?

Nearly 40 percent of us are doing a little less or a lot less. About 30 percent of us are doing about the same amount of exercise as before. The remaining 30 percent say they are doing more.

Women are slightly more likely than men to be exercising. And this time, education doesn't have much to do with it. Whether we have a high school or postgraduate diploma, we are doing slightly less to keep ourselves in shape than we did at thirty.

Amount of Exercise at Forty Compared to Thirty

	Male	Female
	%	%
A lot more	9	13
A little more	15	20
About the same	33	31
A little less	27	21
A lot less	15	15

Red Meat

Red meat has had bad press. Associated with high-fat diets and with the cholesterol scare of the 1970s, it has never fully recovered among forties as a food of choice.

More than half of us eat less red meat now than we did ten years ago. Nearly one-quarter say they eat a lot less. And a few hardy souls (about 5 percent) eat a little or a lot more of it.

There is a relationship between income and education and eating red meat. As your income and your education go up, you are less likely to eat as much red meat as you did ten years ago.

Red Meat Consumption at Forty Compared to Thirty

	Sex		Under	Income $30,000–	$50,000	Education Grade	High	College	Post-
	Male	Female	$30,000	$49,000	plus	School	School		grad
	%	%	%	%	%	%	%	%	%
A lot more	1	1	1	0	1	5	1	1	—
A little more	5	3	5	4	2	5	5	3	2
About the same	45	38	49	41	33	18	17	29	32
A little less	28	32	24	31	36	8	28	34	32
A lot less	22	26	21	24	28	18	17	29	32

Stress

We know stress kills. In fact, we develop stress from hearing about how stressful stress can be. Stress breeds stress. We are a stress-obsessed generation.

Or so the media tell us. Is it true?

At forty, more than half of us have more stress than we did ten years ago. Just over 20 percent are lucky enough to feel less stress. And stress doesn't change with income, education, or the size of the city you live in.

Stress at Forty Compared to Thirty

	Male	Female
	%	%
A lot more	25	26
A little more	27	28
About the same	26	22
A little less	14	13
A lot less	7	10

Top Five Causes of Stress

But what causes stress? The top-five causes identified by forty-year-olds are:

1.	Job	3.	Children	5.	Health
2.	Money	4.	Marriage		

We asked forties what the number-one source of stress was in life.

All of us can name dozens of little things, from waiting in line to being cut-off on the freeway by some lunatic who fails to signal. However, being asked to identify our number-one source of stress forces us to focus on the one item that is most likely to be destructive in our lives.

Jobs lead the list. They are number one for more than half of all men and a third of women.

Money is number two and seems to be a bigger source of stress in small towns than big cities. The less education you have, the more likely money is to be a big source of stress. The more education you have, the more likely the job is to be a big source of stress.

When it comes to home life and children, women carry the burden. Over 22 percent list it as their number-one source of stress, while barely 8 percent of men say it is.

The same is true of marriage. More women than men list marriage as their number-one stress source.

Farther down the list, health problems are a major source of stress for barely 6 percent of forties. To rank as number one, ahead of job, money, and home life, the health problems must be severe.

Number-One Source of Personal Stress

	Sex		Under	Population of City		2 million
	Male	Female	50,000	50,000– 499,000	500,000– 1.99 million	plus
	Male	*Female*	*50,000*	*499,000*	*1.99 million*	*plus*
	%	%	%	%	%	%
Job	53	34	31	43	38	40
Money	22	25	29	23	23	21
Children	8	22	14	16	15	15
Marital	6	12	8	8	9	9
Health	4	7	8	5	6	5

	Income			Education			
	Less than $30,000	*$30,000– $49,000*	*$50,000 plus*	*Grade School*	*High School*	*College*	*Post- graduate*
	%	%	%	%	%	%	%
Job	28	42	46	32	29	43	52
Money	34	21	14	29	28	22	15
Children	13	16	16	16	19	13	7
Marital	9	6	11	8	9	9	9
Health	9	6	3	8	7	4	6

Reducing Stress

With all that stress, what do we do to reduce it?

The number-one choice is physical activity—working it off by working it out. The more education you have, the more likely you are to use physical activity to get rid of stress. This is probably because your job consists of a lot of mental work and sitting at a desk.

The number-two way of reducing stress is through some form of personal activity such as a hobby—gardening, fishing, sewing, camping, and so on. Close to one-quarter of all forties reduce physical stress this way. The more education you have, the less likely you are to reduce stress through these activities.

Number three on the list is good old TV. Nearly 19 percent of us watch TV as our number-one way to reduce stress.

Much farther down the list comes number four. Even though we know we shouldn't, just over 6 percent of us use alcohol, drugs, or tobacco as our first choice to reduce stress. Remember, we asked the respondents to identify their number-one way of reducing stress. That means that, at any given time, among a group of forty-year-olds, close to 300,000 use alcohol, drugs, or tobacco as the number-one way of reducing stress.

Close behind comes reading, followed by meditation and prayer.

In spite of all the talk about taking time for vacations or just to relax and smell the flowers, barely 3 percent of us use this tool as our number-one way of reducing personal stress. In fact, another 2 percent of us work even harder to get rid of stress.

Finally, close to the bottom of our list, we find talking to a friend or eating.

Number-One Way of Reducing Personal Stress

		Sex		Education		
				Grade	High		Post-
		Male	Female	School	School	College	graduate
		%	%	%	%	%	%
1.	Physical activity	28	25	18	23	27	35
2.	Hobby (gardening,fishing, sewing, camping, etc.)	26	23	34	27	25	13
3.	Watch TV	21	17	26	22	16	17
4.	Alcohol/drugs/tobacco	8	5	5	8	6	4
5.	Reading	2	9	3	5	5	7
6.	Meditation/prayer/	3	5	5	4	4	5
7.	Relax/vacation/stress management/solitude	2	4	7	2	3	3
8.	Accomplish tasks/ work harder	1	2	5	1	2	1
9.	Discussion of problems/ visit/talk to a friend	1	3	–	1	3	1
10.	Eat/snacking on food	0	2	–	1	2	1

Chapter 5: Sex

How Often Are You Having Sex at Forty Compared to Thirty?

Almost across the board, we are having sex less often at forty than we did at thirty. Black, white, male, female, rich, poor, educated, uneducated, we are having a little less sex than we did a decade earlier.

Only one group is having sex more often now than ten years ago—unmarried forty-year-olds in a relationship. On the whole, if you are a member of this group, you are having sex a little more often than you did in the past.

Frequency of Having Sex at Forty Compared to Thirty

	Male	Female
	%	%
A lot more	6	9
A little more	15	15
About the same	37	33
A little less	28	25
A lot less	12	15
Don't know/No answer	2	4

Are You Enjoying Sex as Much as You Did Ten Years Ago?

	Male	Female
	%	%
A lot more	20	21
A little more	27	27
About the same	41	34
A little less	7	8
A lot less	3	5
Don't know/No answer	3	5

How Often Do You Have Sex?

We are having sex less often but enjoying it more. But how often is less often?

Most of us (more than 65 percent) had sex within the last week.

A small minority (7 percent) haven't had sex for more than a year. That number as a total doesn't appear surprising, but the details hold some eyebrow-raisers.

For example, among married forty-year-olds, 3 percent haven't had sex for more than a year. Among singles not in a relationship, 26 percent haven't had sex for more than a year.

On the flip side, your likelihood of having had sex within the last week increases with your income and your education. Do schooling and money make you hornier?

The horniest group of all seems to be people who make more than $50,000 a year. Nearly 73 percent of them have had sex within the last week. Who says money can't buy happiness?

Last Time You Had Sex

	Male	Female
	%	%
Less than 1 week ago	67	64
Less than 2 weeks ago	12	11
Less than 1 month ago	6	6
Less than 6 months ago	5	4
Less than 1 year ago	1	1
More than 1 year ago	5	8
Don't know/No answer		

Last Time You Had Sex — Married

	Total %	1st Marriage %	2nd Marriage %	3rd Marriage %
Less than 1 week ago	71	70	72	77
Less than 2 weeks ago	12	12	13	11
Less than 1 month ago	5	7	2	—
Less than 6 months ago	4	5	4	—
Less than 1 year ago	0	0	1	3
More than 1 year ago	3	3	3	3
Don't know/No answer	4	4	4	6

Last Time You Had Sex — Single

	Total %	Separated %	Divorced %	Never married %	In relationship %	Not in relationship %
Less than 1 week ago	48	52	57	37	81	29
Less than 2 weeks ago	9	10	7	12	8	8
Less than 1 month ago	8	—	10	7	4	11
Less than 6 months ago	6	3	5	8	1	9
Less than 1 year ago	5	14	3	4	—	8
More than 1 year ago	18	21	16	20	4	26
Don't know/No answer	6	—	3	12	2	8

Has AIDS Affected Forties' Sexual Behavior?

	Male %	Female %
Much more cautious	38	46
More cautious	44	39
About the same	15	12
Less cautious	0	1
Much less cautious	—	1
Don't know/No answer	3	3

Impotence

Every man has occasional periods of impotence. However, at forty, you have one chance in five of having difficulty getting an erection for a period longer than five weeks.

Chances of Impotence
(for more than five consecutive weeks)

	Age	
30–39	40–49	50–59
%	%	%
13	22	29

Pregnancy

The largest number of women in history are having a first child at forty. What are the odds for men and women of becoming parents at forty?

Chance of a Woman Becoming Pregnant
(per 1,000 women)

	Age	
40–44	45–49	50–54
22.6	4.4	3.4

Chance of a Man Fathering a Child
(per 1,000 men)

	Age	
40–44	45–49	50–54
38.3	14.6	5.8

Chapter 6: Family

Who's Happy?

Whether married or not, close to 90 percent of forties are in a relationship. Although most of these relationships are in marriage, more than 12 percent of forty-year-old women are not married but are in a relationship.

The question is, how happy are we?

The majority of us are very happy, or at least, reasonably happy. But almost 20 percent of forties are just kind of getting along. Their relationship is passable or makes them unhappy.

Feelings about Your Relationship

	Male	Female
	%	%
Very happy	37	34
Happy	32	28
It's okay	13	16
Not happy	3	4
Very unhappy	0	1
Not in a relationship	10	13
Don't know/No answer	4	5

Mom and Dad

As we turn forty, 43 percent of us have lost our fathers. Finally, cruelly, we are experiencing the statistics of the insurance companies. Women are likely to outlive men. Our mothers will live at least six years longer than our fathers. Fewer than 22 percent of us have lost our mothers.

But the numbers add up to one startling statistic: At forty, more than half of us have lost at least one parent. An unfortunate group of us, totaling 12 percent of forties, have lost both parents. Only 47 percent of us have both parents living.

When a parent gets sick or dies, we tend to reevaluate our relationship with our parents. In our teens, most of us thought our parents didn't understand us. With benefit of hindsight, we start to mellow toward our parents.

If we have living parents, we get along with them better than we did ten years ago. About 50 percent of us say we get along with them about the same, but nearly a third of forties say we get along better or much better with our parents than we did ten years ago.

We even like them more. In fact, nearly 30 percent of us like them better or much better and only 6 percent of us like them less than we did ten years ago. (Almost the same percentage said they get along with them worse or much worse.) Age seems to mellow us like a fine wine.

How Do You Get Along with Your Parents Compared to Ten Years Ago?

	Male	Female
	%	%
Much better	10	13
Better	20	23
About the same	51	48
Worse	4	4
Much worse	2	1

Note: Figures do not add up to 100 percent because of deaths among parents.

How Do You Like Your Parents Compared to Ten Years Ago?

	Male	Female
	%	%
Much better	11	13
Better	17	19
About the same	54	50
Less	3	4
Much less	2	2

Note: Figures do not add up to 100 percent because of deaths among parents.

Chapter 8: Regrets

Biggest Regrets

Personal relationships led the list of regrets. When asked what our single biggest regret was at forty, almost a third of us said personal relationships.

Insufficient education was the number-one regret for nearly 20 percent of forties. We have come to recognize that, in this complex, technological world, education opens a lot of doors.

With hindsight, almost 10 percent consider bad career choices to be their number-one regret. A job not taken might mean a dream unpursued.

One out of ten forties have no regrets at all. This is either a result of an extremely fortunate life or a philosophical acceptance of the fact that regrets can't change life, won't make it any better, and often fail to induce positive change.

Top-Six Regrets at Forty

	Male %	Female %
1. Problems with personal relationships	28	38
2. Not enough education	16	19
3. Bad career choices	12	10
4. No regrets	10	10
5. Money/financial	9	8
6. Health	4	5

Regret #1: Personal Relationships

The biggest area for regrets is personal relationships.

Marriage, kids, divorce, the death of a spouse or a close relative—these topped the list for biggest regrets as we turn forty.

The wrong kind of marriage—marrying too early, marrying the wrong person—led the list.

If you're a woman of forty, there's one chance in ten that a bad marriage is your biggest regret in life. If you're a man, the chances are half that.

For every woman who regrets remaining married for too long, there is another who regrets never having married at all.

For every woman who said she had kids too early and wasn't a good mother, there were two who wished they had had more children or that they had had them earlier.

For every woman who said she didn't put enough time into parenting or spend enough time with the kids, there were two men who felt the same way.

The more money you make, the less likely you are to have regrets in personal relationships.

Regret #2: Education

It's not surprising that the biggest regrets about education come from those of us who have only grade school or high school training.

It is surprising that one in ten of those who have postgraduate education say a lack of education is their biggest regret in life so far. Obviously, for some of us, modern life requires increasing levels of special education.

Regret about education doesn't have a lot to do with money. It has a lot more to do with a sense of self-worth and personal esteem. People making more than $50,000 a year were just as likely as people making less than $30,000 a year to regret not having had more education.

Biggest Regret: Insufficient Education

		Population of City			
				500,000–	
Sex		Less than	50,000–	1.99	2 million
Male	Female	50,000	499,000	million	plus
%	%	%	%	%	%
16	19	20	19	16	15

Income			Education			
Less than	$30,000–	$50,000	Grade	High		Post-
$30,000	$49,000	plus	School	School	College	graduate
%	%	%	%	%	%	%
18	17	17	21	21	15	11

Regret #3: Career

Set your goals clearly when you're younger. That is the message of forties whose biggest regret involves their career.

Basically, career regrets centered around a lack of clear goals, the wrong job, working too hard, or not being employed in the field that you want.

The forties' perspective says this about career regrets: set goals early and move to achieve them; work to get a job you like; take time to smell the flowers.

Biggest Regret: Career

	Male	Female
	%	%
Total	12	10
Not attaining goals/not setting and achieving goals/should have defined career objectives more clearly/not gained professional career/poor career moves	5	6

	Males %	Females %
My job/doing what I do/no career/not paying high enough/not successful	5	2
Less of self into job/not working so hard/not taking time to enjoy life	2	1
Leaving my chosen field/not being employed in my field/job I want	1	1

Regret #4: No Regrets

What does it mean to have no regrets as you turn forty? It means that you have accepted life as it comes, that you recognize that life isn't always smooth and that regrets can weigh you down.

If you have no regrets, you are not alone. One in ten forties has none.

No Regrets

Sex		Population of City			
Male	Female	Less than 50,000	50,000– 499,000	500,000– 1.99 million	2 million plus
%	%	%	%	%	%
10	10	11	7	16	8

Income			Education			
Less than $30,000	$30,000– $49,000	$50,000 plus	Grade School	High School	College	Post- graduate
%	%	%	%	%	%	%
10	8	13	11	10	9	11

Regret #5: Money

For most forties, money isn't the biggest regret. Fewer than 10 percent consider it the number-one regret.

A few of us regret not being rich and not getting to do the things we wanted to do because of a lack of money. Almost the same number regret not having bought a house earlier or not having a larger home.

Biggest Regret: Not Enough Money

	Sex		Less than	50,000–	Population of City 500,000– 1.99	2 million
	Male	Female	50,000	499,000	million	plus
	%	%	%	%	%	%
	9	8	8	10	6	10

Income			Education			
Under	$30,000–	$50,000	Grade	High		Post-
$30,000	$49,000	plus	School	School	College	gradate
%	%	%	%	%	%	%
12	8	5	3	11	8	6

Regret #6: Health

Most of us don't consider health our biggest regret.

If we do, we regret having gained weight and gotten out of shape; having abused ourselves with alcohol, cigarettes, and drugs; or having the bad luck to run into an accident or disease.

Forty is a bit young to start having big health regrets. They come later in life.

Chapter 9: Heaven and Hell

Self-Professed Religious Choice

The media have focused heavily on opportunists, fanatics, scheming politicians, and fundamentalist preachers who make political hay out of America's supposed collapse into "Godlessness." Based on this nationwide survey of forties, they couldn't be farther out to lunch.

Fewer than 10 percent of all those surveyed said they had no religion or didn't know what religion they were. Everyone else made a choice.

We asked respondents to check off one of the following: Protestant, Catholic, Jew, none don't know, or other. Many chose to write in their particular religion, ranging from Baptist and Mormon to Buddhist. On the whole, an overwhelming majority of today's forties identified themselves as Protestant or Catholic.

Religious Choice

	Male	Female
	%	%
Protestant	44	44
Catholic	25	27
Jew	3	2
None	8	7
Don't know	3	1
Other	16	18

What Happens after Death

In most cases, religion is a way of dealing with death. The idea of eternal life holds a strong attraction and forms the pillars of Christianity and Islam.

A few billion of the Earth's inhabitants believe in some form of reincarnation in which our souls are sent back to Earth to constantly work out weaknesses which weren't dealt with during this life.

In view of the fact that an overwhelming majority of forties say they are Christians, it's surprising that there is a great deal of uncertainty about what happens after death.

Women are much more likely than men to believe you go to heaven or hell after death.

The smaller the city you live in, the more likely you are to believe in heaven and hell.

The higher your income, the less likely you are to believe in heaven and hell.

The greater your education, the less likely you are to believe in heaven or hell.

What Happens after Death?

Go to heaven or hell	54%
Don't know	23%
Nothing	10%
Versions of reincarnation	8%

Belief in Heaven or Hell

Sex		Less than 50,000	50,000– 499,000	Population of City 500,000– 1.99 million	2 million plus
Male	Female				
%	%	%	%	%	%
49	59	62	62	54	44

Income			Education		
Less than $30,000	$30,000–$00 $49,000	$50,000 plus	High School	College	Post- graduate
%	%	%	%	%	%
58	55	48	57	52	49

About the Author

John Parikhal is one of America's leading authorities on trends, lifestyle, and media. Founder and chief executive officer of Joint Communications, a research and consulting firm, Parikhal has brought his insights and strategies to thousands of individuals, trade associations, and companies throughout the United States and Canada.

To communicate with John Parikhal or to obtain more information about his services and products, contact:

Joint Communications Corp.
90 Burnhamthorpe Road West
Suite 410
Mississauga, Ontario
L5B 3C3
Canada

Phone: (416) 272-1136